Natural Horsemanship Explained

Natural Horsemanship Explained

FROM HEART TO HANDS

Robert M. Miller, D.V.M.
With an introduction by
Patrick Handley, Ph.D.

THE LYONS PRESS
Guilford, Connecticut
An imprint of The Globe Pequot Press

To buy books in quantity for corporate use
or incentives, call **(800) 962–0973**
or e-mail **premiums@GlobePequot.com**.

The Lyons Press is an imprint of The Globe Pequot Press.

10 9 8 7 6 5 4 3 2 1

Printed in the United States of America

Designed by Maggie Peterson

ISBN 978-1-59921-234-0   **3 1088 1005 8881 1**

Library of Congress Cataloging-in-Publication Data is available on file.

To the clinicians, who originated, endorsed,
and passionately taught natural horsemanship,
this book is dedicated.

Beyond what you have done for horsemen and the equine industry, you have been a benefit to man's most loyal and often abused servant, the horse. Even more important, you have proven that reason is a far more effective way to get along with other individuals than is the use of force.

"Great spirits have always encountered violent
opposition from mediocre minds."
—Albert Einstein

"Some people make the same mistake a hundred
times and call it experience."
—Jacob Markowitz (*Canine Surgery*,
The North American Veterinarian, Inc., 1949)

Contents

Acknowledgments

Once again, I express my appreciation to the many clinicians involved in *The Revolution in Horsemanship*.

I am indebted to Rick Lamb, coauthor of the book we published in 2004 bearing that title. This new book, which is a sort of sequel, would not have been written except its predecessor suggested a need for it. Without Rick there may never have been *The Revolution in Horsemanship*.

Thank you, Dorothy Wright, for typing my handwritten manuscripts. Your ability to read my handwriting means that you would have made an effective cryptographer.

I am very grateful to Bill Reynolds, publisher of *Cowboys and Indians* magazine, for his experienced advice, his support, and his encouragement.

Thank you, Pintado, the first colt I ever started, in 1948. The mistakes I made set me off on a lifelong search for a better method. I am truly grateful that I lived long enough to see the establishment of natural horsemanship all over the world.

I must also thank the Californios, the vaqueros who produced the first reined stock horses I had ever seen. I was not a native of California, but in 1947 I went to work as a horse wrangler on the historic Irvine Ranch. It was my first exposure to the concept of lightness, and it led me to a search to understand how it was achieved.

Lastly, my thanks to my wife and partner of fifty years, Debby, who provided so many of the illustrations in this book and was helpful in so many other ways, and to my son, Mark, whose assistance and encouragement were invaluable.

Foreword

As a lifelong horse lover and behavioral psychologist, I admit it—I'm addicted to horse training seminars, books, and videos. I love learning from the experts, the so-called horse whisperers. I've seen some of these talented individuals over and over again and I continue to be amazed and entertained by what they do and the results they get. But sometimes I flinch when I hear some of them use psychological terms incorrectly. Words like negative reinforcement, punishment, successive approximation, shaping, and so on, have specific scientific meanings and, when used carelessly or inappropriately, it not only confuses the audience, it also misrepresents the field of behavioral psychology. However, a solution is at hand!

Who better to explain in scientific terms what horse whisperers really do and why horses respond to them the way they do, than Dr. Robert Miller.

When I was first introduced to Dr. Miller, I was a bit taken aback to meet someone in an entirely different vocation who had so much knowledge about my specialty area. In my opinion, Dr. Robert Miller deserves an honorary PhD in psychology, for he not only understands behavioral psychology, but its application specifically to the horse. He accurately identifies what it is that really works in the techniques of those talented trainers who have been labeled "horse whisperers."

Actually, those who make their livings conducting horse-training seminars, the ones so often labeled "horse whisperers," have no better friend than Bob Miller. He credits them with the breakthrough revolution in schooling horses in ways natural to the horse, not the human. Miller acknowledges all that they contribute, yet reveals to the reader the science behind their achievements so that even those of us who are less talented can understand and appreciate their techniques.

As an animal vet and surgeon, years ago Dr. Miller mastered the skill of operating on tumors and stitching up cuts. But he has also developed the skill of dissecting perplexing psychological behavioral chains that lead to desirable and undesirable horse behaviors. He knows what really happens behind a whisper. It's often not what you think at all.

The chapter on predatory behavior, as distinctly different from the predator-prey model, is worth the price of the book alone. It wonderfully clarifies why certain behaviors, regardless of who or what is demonstrating them, create fear in the horse. You'll be enlightened!

The magic and the secret of understanding "horse whispering" is in identifying what is really working and what isn't. It's all related to operant conditioning, reward schedules, negative reinforcement, consequence timing, and other techniques that sound complex, but which we can easily learn. Now here's what's exciting.

Dr. Miller's insights and humorous stories help us understand why it is behavioral psychology, not magic or horse-whispering secrets, that brings about change in the horse. Plus, this book is written for everyone. It's engaging enough for the beginner and in-depth enough for the seasoned rider and advanced trainer.

Of course, a book is useless unless people read it. No problem! Once you start this book, you'll finish it. Dr. Miller magically gains our attention and keeps it even when describing very complex technical information by weaving together simple explanations and fascinating examples from his years of experience, all the while peppering these with his homespun sense of humor. You'll laugh and learn all at the same time.

Although focusing on what professional trainers do to get results, Dr. Miller also credits and applauds all those backyard horse owners who have taken the trail less traveled and chosen to use gentle, persuasive methods for developing their horses. They have been the silent foot soldiers of horse whispering who have really made the difference in the revolution. Many have used some of the techniques Dr. Miller describes without even realizing it. They'll learn how much they instinctively knew all along, what to continue doing, and new things to try for achieving even better results.

The only person who, because of his own personal humility, receives little credit in this book is Dr. Miller himself. Recently inducted into the Western States Horse Expo Hall of Fame, Dr. Miller has taken the concepts of natural horsemanship and early learning to millions of people through his own veterinary career, articles, books, and speaking engagements. He's been whispering all along, and readers are in for a treat to learn once again from a legend in the field.

So close your lips and whisper to your horse-loving friends, "Get Dr. Miller's newest book, *Natural Horsemanship Explained*. And read it soon!"

—Patrick Handley, PhD

About Dr. Handley

Dr. Patrick Handley is a licensed psychologist specializing in organizational behavioral management. He received his PhD in personality assessment and organizational behavior from the University of Missouri in 1980. He also had the privilege of studying behavioral management under Dr. Aubrey Daniels, a longtime student of B. F. Skinner, one of the founders of behaviorism.

Dr. Handley's career in organizational consulting has focused for more than fifteen years on behavioral performance improvement—how to utilize the concepts of behavior change, motivation, and consequence delivery to improve workplace performance.

Dr. Handley grew up on a small farm in northwestern Missouri where he developed a love for horses. He has fond memories of his father picking corn by hand as he rode in a wagon behind two huge draft horses. Later as a youth he rode in 4-H competitions and has since owned and shown horses most of his adult life.

Introduction

In our last book, *The Revolution in Horsemanship*, coauthored with Rick Lamb, we described the history and the philosophy of the phenomenal movement that has swept the horse industry, one that is changing the methods by which we humans communicate with and shape the behavior of one of the animal species we have successfully domesticated, the horse.

Throughout human history there have been occasional horsemen with the perception, the empathy, the sensitivity, the compassion, the patience, and the skill to master the optimum methods of communicating with horses. But not until the last quarter of the twentieth century when, ironically, the horse had become a primarily recreational and companion animal, did these methods become widespread and adopted by horse owners and trainers en masse. Around 1980, the historical movement had arrived due to a number of factors: In the industrialized nations the typical horse owner was educated. A century earlier a large percentage of the people working with horses were uneducated, or even illiterate. This situation persists in undeveloped cultures to this very day.

The information explosion, including videography, the Internet, television, books, and motion pictures had a major effect, as did the clinicians who, often traveling internationally by jet aircraft, spread the word.

An increasing public awareness of animal welfare and human relationships with animals encouraged the movement, which, surprisingly, was furthered not by world-class masters of classical horsemanship, but by a small group of working cowboys from the Pacific Northwestern region of the United States. Filled with evangelical zeal, these cowboys, most of them veteran rodeo competitors as well as working ranch hands, launched a revolution that is known today most commonly as "natural horsemanship," although numerous other names have been given to it, all of them quite appropriately descriptive of the method. Undoubtedly, this revolution would not have occurred as soon as it did were it not that, for the first time in human history, the horse industry in Western civilization was being increasingly dominated by women. Men from the working cowboy culture may have launched the revolution, but women enabled it to prosper and grow.

All of this is thoroughly described in *The Revolution in Horsemanship*. Additionally, the subtitle of the book, *And What It Means to Mankind*, indicates that it also deals with a more extensive impact of the revolution.

Briefly, we suggested that if by learning and using optimum communication methods emphasizing persuasion rather than coercion, such totally disparate creatures as man—the ultimate predator—and the horse—the ultimate prey—could develop powerful and lasting relationships, why couldn't the same methods better human relationships? These could include the relationships between parent and child, teacher and student, employer and employee, law enforcer and citizen. This dominance—this leadership—is too often imposed coercively through threat, force, and sometimes abuse. But dominance can also be established benevolently through persuasive methods motivated by kindness, understanding, and convincing the subordinate individual that a better way exists.

Personally, in *The Revolution in Horsemanship*, I targeted the uninitiated: those horsepeople who were unfamiliar with the natural horsemanship movement; those who were aware of it but who were complacent, disinterested, and satisfied with traditional techniques; and those who frankly rejected it because it wasn't "macho" or it was too effeminate, or because they believed that "you gotta show the horse who's boss"; and those who were simply satisfied with traditional methods "because they do work." We do indeed need to show the horse "who is boss," but *how* that is done varies tremendously among the various forms of traditional horsemanship and what we have labeled as natural horsemanship. What is natural to the horse is often very unnatural to us.

In this book we target the believers: that ever increasing majority of horse handlers who want a better way; who seek it; who spend time and money to learn it; who want, above all, to be able to relate to the horse like a Ray Hunt, a Pat Parelli, a Dennis Reis, a Chris Cox, a Richard Shrake, or any of their contemporary masters of horsemanship.

We are targeting not only the students of these talented and revolutionary horsemen—and not only their disciples, their protégés, their aficionados, their devoted followers—but also the clinicians themselves.

Too often the students and the teachers themselves do not fully understand the scientific basis for the success of their methods. Understanding the instinctive behavior of both our own species and the horse is essential to understand why persuasive methods are superior to coercive methods in the equine species. Every creature, including humans, is born with certain behavioral traits that are genetically fixed. We must understand these if we are really to comprehend why horses do what they do and why we do what we do. This book emphasizes the reasons why we, as a reasoning species, must often suppress and modify our instinctive human behavior in order to best communicate with horses, because it is unreasonable to ask them, as a reacting species, to alter their behavior to suit us.

Conversely, it is imperative that we understand the scientific principles of behavioral science if we expect to obtain optimum responses from horses to the training techniques we impose upon them.

CHAPTER ONE

What the Revolution Can Mean to Us

In *The Revolution in Horsemanship*, Rick Lamb and I included chapters on the implications that this technological change may have upon human behavior in general. This is why we subtitled our book, *And What It Means to Mankind*. We were not so myopic as to suggest that horses or horsemanship are of any major importance in today's world. However, the essence of natural horsemanship contains a lesson that is enormously significant in human relationships.

No more naturally incompatible species can be found than the horse and human. Consider both from a zoological viewpoint.

Man is a hunter. He is the consummate hunter, not because he is a strict carnivore like a lion, a tiger, or a hawk, but because he is endowed with a reasoning brain, and a body constructed for the use of tools. He walks erect, freeing his hands for tool use. Those hands are equipped with dexterous fingers and an opposable thumb, unlike other related primates. This makes man a deadly hunter.

The horse, on the other hand, must be regarded as the ultimate prey creature. Unlike most other grazing herbivores that serve as prey for the large carnivores such as members of the cat or dog family, the horse does not have anatomical weapons like cattle, sheep, goats, and antelope,

Two veterinary students named Bob Miller on two Morgan horses named Caesar ("Big Caesar" on the left is the sire of "Little Caesar" on the right). We Bobs cowboyed together during the summers. This snapshot was taken at a steer roping competition in Wyoming in 1954. Please note that my horse (right) has no bridle. I am competing at a rodeo on a horse wearing a halter. This was two decades before The Revolution in Horsemanship.

which are horned species. Even the rhinoceros, the hippopotamus, and the elephant fall prey to lions, but let us regard the formidable weapons with which they are equipped.

All of these prey animals utilize flight, but they can and do also use their horns or tusks for defense. The horse, however, is purely a flight creature. Horses will instinctively run, as a herd, away from any intimidating stimulus that suggests predation. The rustling of tall grass as a lion warily stalks grazing horses creates an alarm reaction. This, of course, is why horses, especially young and inexperienced horses, are so jittery and apprehensive on a windy day when leaves and grass are in motion, and why a billowing plastic tarpaulin on a haystack precipitates shying.

Therefore, if a human uses the body language of the horse, understands its reactions and mentality, and can quickly cause the horse to regard him or her as: a) a leader, b) a friend, and c) a trusted companion, then a remarkable bond will be accomplished.

As described in our previous book, even captured mustangs, which have never had previous contact with a human being, can be gentled and made rideable in several hours with natural horsemanship methods. What a remarkable achievement, considering the violent and brutal methods used to subjugate mustangs in the past: roping them, choking them down, biting their ears, blindfolding them, and finally bucking them out to the point of total exhaustion and surrender. How many men and how many horses have been injured or killed in the past using such methods? What were the psychological effects?

Whether we are dealing with horses, with other animals, or with our fellow humans, there are two methods of obtaining subordination and compliance: coercion and persuasion. Throughout human history, both methods have been used.

Coercion requires the threat of force, or actual use of force. Is it effective? Yes! But, is it a civilized method?

Persuasion requires the art of communication. It involves psychological manipulation. If the behavior of the individual, human, or animal is successfully manipulated, then it does what is wanted without developing an attitude of antipathy, resentment, fear, or distrust. This is why the philosophy of natural horsemanship is so important, and why its significance goes far beyond our relationship with horses.

Consider the self-discipline, the emotional control, the concentration that the original clinicians must have had in order to master natural horsemanship. These men were young, working cowboys from the Pacific Northwest. Talk about a macho culture! Nearly all of them were veterans of the rodeo circuit, the rough and tumble cowboy sport. What talent and dedication it took to discipline themselves never to show aggression to a horse, never to become angry, and to control haste, impatience, and frustration.

This is why all the clinicians with whom we have discussed this subject insist that what the horse taught them has improved their relations with their fellow man, including their families. Let me use myself as an example. I am an impatient and kinetic individual. I am in constant motion and in a hurry. Horses taught me patience. I learned that if I took the time it takes, it took less time. I am not very observant. Horses taught me how to focus on an individual and absorb every nuance in that individual's behavior.

I have always been kind and tolerant. Horses reinforced my kindness, because they *appreciate* it. I have always disliked conflict, and horses proved to me that discourse is far superior to conflict for resolving differences. Consider the history of human warfare. After the conflict, killing, destruction, and suffering, only *then* do we sit down at the table and compromise. *Then* we resort to discourse. I am not a pacifist, however. I recognize that when an aggressive individual refuses discourse and is violent, then we must defend ourselves. As a World War II veteran, I am keenly aware that sometimes force is our only option.

Horsemanship is an ancient art. It developed over a period of millennia. Yes, there were always those rare gifted individuals who used methods we now call natural horsemanship, but never before have horsemen the world over accepted it and been transformed by it. From now on, persuasion will rule. Coercion will remain the method of choice

Chris Cox, an amazingly talented horseman and clinician, is shown here working with a foal.

for those whose personality, intellect, and temperament preclude the use of natural horsemanship.

This revolution, as I see it, has two elements. Although neither one is original, and both have been employed before, to use them to completely replace traditional colt-breaking and horse-training methods is indeed revolutionary. These two methods are: 1) The training of baby foals, and 2) The employment of natural horsemanship for training mature horses.

We acknowledge that these are two separate concepts, neither dependent upon the other. Foals are precocial as a species, and as we will describe in a later chapter, they learn more readily in infancy than at any other time of life. However, foals can be trained shortly after birth and develop lasting respect for and trust in humans. Then, after maturity, they can be trained with completely conventional, traditional methods.

Conversely, foals can be given little or no training, or training may be postponed until much later or even until full maturity, but then natural horsemanship can develop a good useable horse.

The two methods are independent, but the optimum method for training horses utilizes both. First, train the horse to shape certain desirable behaviors and attitudes as early in life as possible. Then, building upon that foundation, use natural horsemanship to train the mature young horse to prepare for its life's work.

Horses learn all through life, just as we do. Wild mustangs that have been captured learn to be safe and efficient saddle horses. Horses of middle age never before handled by humans can be—and have been—gentled and made into reliable mounts. However, to ignore the fact that horses are at the peak of their learning abilities during the days and weeks right after their births is to ignore scientific fact and to stubbornly cling to archaic traditions.

Dr. Patricia Luttgen is a veterinarian in Lakewood, Colorado, who raises, trains, and rides warmblood horses. For many years she has "imprint trained" her newborn foals with consistent success. However, she imprint trained one filly and then did not start her afterwards. When the filly had grown into a twelve-year-old unbroken mare, she was introduced to a surcingle, and then a saddle, a bit, and a bridle, all uneventfully. Then Dr. Luttgen simply got on her and commenced riding. No domestic animal learns faster or has better memory than does the horse.

Patricia Luttgen, DVM and her Trakehner mare, Mandalina. This mare was imprint trained at birth and schooled on the ground, but never ridden until 12 years of age when Dr. Luttgen simply got on her and rode.

Here, again, the most important lesson to be learned is not how it applies to horsemanship, but how it relates to human behavior. We know that not only horses but all the species we work with have, early in their lives, critical learning times preprogrammed in their brains. In *altricial* species (those with delayed development, such as cats, dogs, and humans), these periods during which learning occurs with great speed and permanence happen gradually, over a period of time. In puppies this time is from perhaps six to sixteen weeks of age. In humans, the longest lived of all mammals, maturation is very slow, and the critical periods are stretched out over a number of years.

In *precocial* species the newborn must follow a mother and the group in order to stay alive. The critical learning times are compressed into a very brief period beginning at birth. Indeed, it has been shown that learning even occurs before birth. The unborn, for example, learn to recognize certain sounds. So, geese and ducks, quail and turkeys, sheep and cattle, deer and goats—and horses—(note that these are all prey species) are all born precocial.

Whether in precocial or altricial species, the critical learning times occur in babyhood and in childhood.

All of these recently discovered aspects of behavioral science have been proven in recent decades. What is interesting is that we are using this knowledge to achieve amazing results in animals. Horses are learning remarkable things right after birth. Livestock producers are using the same techniques, although simplified, to produce gentle and cooperative animals. Dog trainers are teaching puppies things that were traditionally taught after maturity. Wild animal trainers are working with newborn precocial species to obtain results hitherto thought impossible.

Thus, we are making remarkable progress with animals. But we are losing it with our children. In our modern-day urbanized, mechanized, and completely unnatural society, parenting is becoming a lost art. An alarming percentage of our children are growing up deprived of a full-time family structure. Discipline is untaught. Values are distorted, important ones being ignored and frivolous ones being emphasized. The effects of television, most of which ranges from mindless trash to devastatingly damaging sewage, is shaping the thinking, the values, and the behavior of millions of children.

We can take a newborn foal, and with several hours of work, teach it to trust us, to depend upon us, to emulate us, to respond to our direction.

The extraordinary show, "Cavalia," originating in Montreal, Canada, tours the world. Trainer and star of the show, Frederique Pignon, works his mature stallions at liberty, demonstrating complete control. Nothing separates the horses from the audience or keeps the horse from leaving. Using natural horsemanship methods, Pignon achieves absolute respect without fear from the stallions.

We can take a puppy, and with a few weeks of work, shape its behavior and socialize it for the rest of its life.

Similarly, we can take a child, and surrounding it with positive stimuli, learning opportunities, love, affection, and encouragement, produce a well balanced, reasonable, compassionate, and productive human being. Some parents are still doing this. Regrettably, others are producing children who are rude, selfish, vain, shallow, and lacking goals, discipline, or a sound moral code. Worse, millions of children in this world are being schooled to hate, and all mankind suffers as a result.

The *power* of early learning is awesome. With it we can produce a more civilized society, or a culture of savagery. This is one of the most vital lessons the revolution in horsemanship can offer all mankind.

CHAPTER TWO

The Mind/Feet Connection

I am well known for teaching the technique of training newborn foals, which I called imprint training because it is ideally done during the imprinting period. Imprinting—the instinct for the newborn to bond with what it sees moving around it—occurs immediately following birth in the horse, a precocial prey species. The horse is born with all senses fully functional, neurologically mature, with full learning capacity, and capable of keeping up with its dam and the herd in flight from danger. This is in contrast to altricial species, such as dogs, cats, or humans. In these species the newborn are helpless, dependent, with all senses only partially developed. They are neurologically immature, the critical learning times for imprinting and socialization are delayed, and learning in general is quite limited.

Imprint training will be discussed more fully later in this book. Other than giving it a name, ritualizing the training procedure, and promoting its use, I did not originate anything. Certain individuals, and certain cultures, have advocated training newborn foals in the past. I may have popularized it, but I certainly didn't invent it.

Nevertheless, the popularity, simplicity, and effectiveness of foal training have led to a second career for a veterinarian who retired from a successful and very rewarding practice at the age of sixty in 1987.

Soon after that retirement began, an unplanned career teaching equine behavior was launched, primarily because of the popularity of the books and tapes I produced about foal training.*

However, a more important contribution is the concept that the dominance hierarchy in horses is established by controlling the movement of one's peers. Let's elucidate that concept because, although I have not read of it elsewhere, I believe that the entire success of the natural horsemanship movement is due to the utilization of that fact: that dominance (leadership) is determined in the equine species not by force, superior strength, or the infliction of physical damage, but by dominant individuals controlling the movement of subordinate individuals. This doesn't mean that horses do not fight, or that they do not inflict injury upon other horses by kicking, striking, and biting. We all know that they do. But wild horse herds generally are led by an older, sometimes even a somewhat decrepit mare. Although not by any means the strongest or the most dangerous individual in the herd, she is most effective at controlling the movement of the other horses.

Movement is life to the horse, a flight creature. Unlike so many prey animals that have effective weapons of defense, the horse lacks the horns of cattle, the horn on the nose of a rhinoceros, or the tusks of elephants, swine, or hippopotami. Horses survive by running away from any stimulus—visual, olfactory, auditory, or tactile—that is unfamiliar and that they interpret as dangerous (a *novel stimulus*). If their escape proves successful, in their view, then they quickly learn to use flight to escape that same stimulus once it is again presented. That's why some horses are afraid of plastic, flags, umbrellas, pigs, donkeys, bicycles, or electric clippers. They were once frightened by that stimulus and now believe that they successfully fled it.

The horse is frightened by an initial experience, remembers it, repeats it subsequently, and learns to escape with a flight reaction. The flight response is not necessarily running away. It may be partial flight reaction like throwing the head, shying, or a sudden evasive movement.

---

* Video: *Imprint Training of the Foal*, Palomine Productions, 1984
Book: *Imprint Training of the Newborn Foal*, Western Horseman, 1991
Video: *Early Learning*, Video Velocity, 1995

The results are the countless "ear shy" horses, "goosey" horses, chronic shyers and "spookers," horses who won't allow a foot to be picked up or a temperature to be taken, who refuse to accept the bit, or who are afraid of any variety of things including llamas, farriers, and veterinarians.

The horse's behavior is closely linked to its anatomy and physiology. This is true of every animal that successfully survives in its natural habitat. All three—behavior, anatomy, and physiology—must be conducive to survival as a species. If the habitat changes, then these qualities must also change or the species will become extinct. It is important to remember that the horse originated in North America, descended from a smaller swamp-dwelling predecessor. It evolved, adapting to grassy plains, surviving predation by saber-toothed cats, lions, and huge wolves, and by man, only to become extinct about 12,000 years ago.

Fortunately, by that time, the horse had long ago crossed the Bering Strait land bridge into Asia, from where it migrated into the Middle East, Europe, and Africa. From there the horse further evolved into a variety of related equine species such as the ass, the onager, and the zebra, as well as a variety of wild horses. All species of the family Equidae are well designed to cope with a grazing environment populated with a variety of hungry predators.

Horses in a group have the best chance to survive in nature. They are highly sociable herd animals. The leader of the herd, usually an older mare, maintains her authority by controlling the movement of the rest of the group. She uses threatening body language to inhibit or to cause movement by the other horses in the group. She decides when to flee, in which direction to flee, and how far to go. The subordinate horses follow her. When the group flees, they all go together. By contrast the stallion that presides over the harem of mares is in charge of reproduction. He is usually younger than the lead mare because once past his prime he will be forced out by a younger and stronger stallion. He will then go off to live his final days in a bachelor band. When the group flees, the stallion runs in back, harassing the stragglers and urging them to keep up with the lead mare.

Horses, like other animals that live in groups, will accept a surrogate. That is, they will accept a substitute creature to bond with just as they will bond with their own kind. Isn't that why we become so attached to our pets? They become surrogate children, surrogate grandchildren, surrogate friends, even surrogate slaves, and occasionally, surrogate masters. Therefore, human beings, understanding and mimicking the body language of horses, can do what horses do. We can control the movement of the subject horse, and by doing so, establish ourselves in the horse's mind as a herd leader. If the horse views us completely as a herd leader, as a dominant horse, we gain trust, dependency, a desire to follow us (even if we are on the horse's back), a need to be close to us, and, above all, the same respect for us that it would have for a dominant mare.

The goal should be total respect and zero fear. Traditional horsemanship techniques work, but they are rarely devoid of fear, and rarely produce complete respect. Yet that is an attainable goal, and the leading natural horsemanship clinicians repeatedly demonstrate this truth, often with rebellious, spoiled, and intractable horses.

CHAPTER THREE

The Key to Leadership

If we control the horse's feet, we control its mind. If we control movement, we dominate the horse. If the horse learns that we can cause it to move, or, conversely, inhibit its movement, it will signal with gestures of its head and its mouth that it accepts us as its leader. It will lick and chew and lower its head.

This sequence will be clear when we regard the various traditional ways we humans have learned to dominate the horse.

We *restrain* movement by teaching horses to stand tied. We call this technique "halter breaking." The horse tamers of past centuries changed dangerous outlaw horses with remarkable speed by controlling flight. They cast them on their sides and did not allow them to rise. They confined them to stocks. They even mounted them while swimming in deep rivers. Unable to run, the horses would accept the riders by the time they reached shore. Green colts were snubbed up to a well-trained lead horse. Hind legs were tied up. All sorts of hobbles have been used to abort flight. Forelegs are hobbled, at the fetlock in North America and above the knees in Australia. Hind legs are hobbled in Argentina. Three legs have been hobbled and even four legs.

The "running W," a device by which both forelegs can be suddenly restrained by the human handler, dropping the horse to its knees, has a profound effect in creating submissiveness.

A colt, tied head to tail, learns to flex laterally and bend the body. It also becomes submissive because its ability to flee is compromised.

In recent years wild mustangs have been captured, confined in a chute, and buried in sand or grain to induce submissiveness by depriving the subject of instinctive flight. Heads have been tied to tails so the horse could only circle, and not run away. Even blindfolding horses, a long-used technique for gentling refractory individuals, is effective because if a horse cannot see, its ability to flee is compromised.

I do not necessarily condone these practices. I simply list them to illustrate how extensively flight deprivation has been used in the past to induce submission.

Conversely, we can *cause* movement in a horse, just as the herd leader does by laying her ears back and swiftly gesturing aggressively toward a subordinate. The subordinate, responding by moving *away* from the leader, acknowledges her dominance. It is the equivalent of a human salute, or bow to a superior.

Consider how many techniques are used to train horses that involve *causing* movement. We longe them on a confining line, or drive them in long lines. We free-longe them in a round pen. We teach them to lead, to back, and to turn in hand by means of a halter shank. We drive them in harness alongside an older well-broke horse. At various times, green horses have been put on carousel-like machines that compel them to move in a constant circle.

There is an important difference between natural horsemanship and traditional horsemanship. Because of human nature, we are inclined to use maximum stimuli to control movement. We'll discuss this aspect of human nature later in this book. By contrast, natural horsemanship utilizes minimal stimuli to control movement, at least initially. Then, if the desired response is not obtained, the intensity of the stimulus is progressively increased.

Thus, for example, a traditional trainer may use a whip to strike a horse being taught to move in a round pen. Today's natural horseman will try first to elicit movement by simply waving a rope, a flag, or a stick, and not by striking the horse except as a last resort.

Similarly, a traditional horseman may induce a horse to back up by sharply jerking on the lead rope, reins, or lines. The modern natural horseman will teach a horse to back by gently wiggling the lead rope, only increasing the force if there is no response, creating a gradually increasing level of discomfort until a step backward is obtained. Thereupon he instantly stops the discomfort, thereby rewarding the horse for its response.

The advantage of using minimum discomfort initially to control movement, and only increasing it *if there is no response*, is that the horse will eventually respond to the minimum signal. It becomes conditioned to automatically respond to the smallest signal possible. This, as we will explain later, is the best way to obtain *lightness*.

When I started veterinary practice, the bread and butter of equine medicine was deworming through a nasogastric tube. A flexible tube was passed up one nostril to the back of the throat, where it was swallowed and then passed into the stomach. The medication was then pumped into the tube. Modern deworming oral pastes and gels had not been developed. The horses were usually restrained for this process by applying a twitch to the upper lip. We were taught this method in our schools and it was universally accepted. Frequently a horse would strike out with its forelegs. When I realized that eventually my luck would run out and I

In Pat Parelli's Yo-Yo Game, he wiggles the lead rope until the horse backs up, where-upon he instantly stops moving the rope, giving the horse instant comfort. Only if the horse doesn't move backward does the rope wiggling intensify. Ultimately the horse learns to back up at the slightest signal; even the wiggling of a finger. The result is respect. Horses in nature rarely back up.

would be injured, I started using the Rarey leg strap. I had learned about the strap in John S. Rarey's nineteenth-century book, *Horse-Taming by a New Method*, before I went to veterinary school. My purpose was simply to disable the leg closest to me, and spoil the horse's aim. I used the leg strap—or "one-leg hobble," as I called it—on any horse I suspected would be inclined to strike.

In time, I noticed an interesting phenomenon. When I removed the tube from the horse's nose, and the twitch was released, most horses moved abruptly *away* from me. Still haltered, it was a modified flight reaction. Those horses wearing a leg strap, however (and remember, these were the more difficult patients), often lowered their heads and moved *closer* to me when the twitch and leg strap were removed. Their eyes had softened. Their lips were parted, a submissive sign. *Something was happening!* It took me many years to figure it out.

The Rarey Leg Strap, created by Ohio horse tamer John Rarey in the 19th century, was used to produce submissiveness.

Taking one leg away from the horse did not merely disable it physically, it changed its attitude toward me, even though I had done unpleasant things to it. It had become *deferential* toward me. It *forgave* me. Although I did not yet comprehend *why* it had changed its attitude toward me, it made me realize that *our* attitudes are the reason most horses can be difficult patients.

I abandoned the routine twitching of horses for doctoring. I switched to a smaller tube to which I could desensitize the horse more quickly, and also tried to make a stroking procedure out of deworming. I learned that many horses can be patiently trained to actually enjoy the procedure because horses are a mutually grooming species that can learn to enjoy any tactile stimulus just so long as it causes no discomfort or pain.

During those early years of practice another thing occurred that made me realize that inhibiting movement led to bonding with and control of horses. In veterinary school my physiology professor, Dr. Donald Rankin, experimented with a drug called succinylcholine. It was manufactured by Squibb, and its proprietary name was Sucostrin. This drug, administered in an exactly proper dose intravenously, completely paralyzed a horse for several minutes. Although the horse was immobilized in a prone position, it was fully conscious but could not move.

After I received my doctorate in veterinary medicine, Dr. Rankin was hired by Squibb to do research and develop a variety of veterinary drugs. I had only been in practice a few weeks in Arizona when he telephoned me and asked if I would like to do clinical trials for him, starting with Sucostrin. I jumped at the opportunity, and during the next twenty years

This is a mule wearing a "tapa ojos," a blindfold used in Latin America in order to inhibit movement. Unable to see, equines are discouraged from using flight. The blindfold is used to calm fearful animals and keep loose stock from running off.

I immobilized 2,500 horses with Sucostrin. Some of these were minor surgery cases, in which we would combine the paralytic drug with a local anesthetic or a systemic pain reliever. But many times I would immobilize a difficult horse simply to facilitate a routine procedure such as tube deworming, minor dentistry, or perhaps a bandage change.

What was remarkable about this was that after I performed the procedure, I found that once the drug wore off and the horse had regained its feet, I could do the same procedure without difficulty. Immobilized but fully conscious, some profound change took place in the horse. It would tolerate without resisting the same procedure that only a few minutes earlier had required either drastic restraint or dramatic medication. Why? What suddenly made these difficult patients completely cooperative?

I finally realized that both the leg strap and the Sucostrin restricted movement and produced submissiveness. *This* is how horses determine their dominance hierarchy, how leadership is determined in the horse: by control of movement.

Silke Valentin, a German mother of 3, was paralyzed in a highway accident. A Pat Parelli student, she has complete control over her huge Friesian horses, shown here riding without a bridle, strapped into the saddle. The horses regard her as an absolute leader as she trains them from a wheel chair. What more dramatic proof exists that physical strength has nothing to do with control of the horse.

Now the methods that were used by the historic horse tamers made sense. John Rarey used his leg strap. Nineteenth-century horse tamer Dennis Magner used a head-to-tail tie and circled the horse, and Professor Beery used a "running W hitch." Generations of American cowboys used the technique of laying a difficult horse down and "tarping" it with a tarpaulin, slapping it vigorously.

Therefore, less extreme but more traditional methods that cause or inhibit movement now became understandable. To a greater or lesser degree, they create an attitude of subordination, a willingness to follow.

Most important, the rationale behind the methods introduced by Tom Dorrance, popularized by Ray Hunt, and emulated by a host of clinicians like Pat Parelli, Bryan Neubert, Chris Cox, Buck Brannaman and so many others became obvious: *Subtle signals that motivate the horse to move or to stand still have a powerful effect. They allow the human controlling the movement of the horse to become a leader in the horse's mind!*

The efficacy of what we have come to call natural horsemanship suddenly became comprehensible. The success of the revolution in horsemanship became entirely predictable.

CHAPTER FOUR

Horses Are Not Afraid of Predators

We hear a lot of talk about the fact that the horse, an herbivore, is a prey species, and, that the human, a partially carnivorous species, is a predator. Because the horse's primary survival behavior is flight, whereas many prey species are actually very aggressive (such as a Spanish fighting bull, or a Cape buffalo), we may consider the horse the *ultimate prey animal*.

Conversely, even though humans are omnivorous, and only partially carnivorous, we may be the *ultimate predator*. Why? Because our reasoning ability and our use of tools (weapons) make us the most effective of all hunters.

We marvel that two such disparate species can develop a powerful bond and interdependent relationship. Yet, it is easily explainable.

Horses are not afraid of predators. They are afraid of predatory behavior.

Years ago, Ringling Brothers and Barnum & Bailey Circus featured a liberty act in which a tiger and a horse worked together, the tiger actually riding upon the horse's back. How was such a thing possible? Isn't the horse instinctively afraid of such a predatory beast as a tiger? No! Horses are afraid of predatory *behavior* or anything they interpret as predatory behavior. We all have seen videos of zebra grazing close to lions in repose. Not until the lions arise and assume a predatory posture do the zebra react.

We humans are a predatory species, yet children and women generally elicit much less fear in horses than do men. Why? Because the male stance, the male posture, the male voice—the total male attitude— are interpreted by the horse as more threatening. Horses don't *reason*. They don't think "That is a predator and I must flee." Horses *react*. "If it seems to be predatory, I must flee. If a piece of paper flying through the air seems to be predatory, I must flee. If an unfamiliar *prey* species acts predatory, I must flee. If I see a llama for the first time and it *may* be predatory, I take no chances. I flee. If I see an umbrella, might it be a predator?"

Predatory behavior takes two forms: the *stalk* and *the charge*. Either elicits flight in the horse. Watch the lion stalk the zebra. Its eyes are intently fixed upon its prey. It crouches, motionless, then advances with slow, deliberate movements. It is *menacing*. A pointer dog, pointing a game bird, does the same thing. So does a border collie working sheep. Even a stallion, a *prey* animal, assumes that head-lowered, fixed gaze predatory posture when driving his band of mares and foals. So, an unfamiliar stump or any unidentified stationary object can alarm a horse and provoke shying, which is a flight response.

Now, consider the charge. When the lion feels it is close enough to overtake the zebra, it charges at sprinting speed. The equines' only chance for

Good sheepdogs assume a stalking pose and fix their gaze upon the livestock they work. This predatory posture intimidates sheep or cattle.

survival is immediate top-speed flight. Similarly, when anything unfamiliar abruptly moves toward the horse—even if it is a nonliving thing such as a flapping sheet of plastic, an unfamiliar vehicle, or a flag or a rope waved by a clinician—it induces flight. Flight ensures survival for horses in the wild.

Monty Roberts' "Join-Up" routine is a classic example of how predatory behavior can affect equine behavior. Initially he acts "predatory": Eyes on eyes, shoulders facing the horse, he stalks. Then, he tosses a line toward the horse. This is a "charge." The horse flees. He pursues. The horse flees for several minutes. It cannot escape. It signals surrender. The ear and eye closest to the threat are fixed on it. In horse language it pleads for help, for leadership, when it chews and licks its lips and lowers its head.

Eventually, Monty abruptly changes his stance. He becomes passive. He is a predator but his behavior is no longer predatory. The horse approaches him apprehensively. Still avoiding eye contact, still passive, he quietly reaches out to stroke the horse.

Eureka! The bond is created, a herd leader and a herd follower. They are joined.

Kell Jeffery was a man ahead of his time. Early in the twentieth century, the young Australian was sent to an outback cattle station for his health. There he conceived of a method of starting and training horses, which we now know as natural horsemanship. Unfortunately, society was not yet ready for the revolution in horsemanship, and, were it not for a few enlightened protégés, he may have been forgotten. Jeffery died in his eighties, an unappreciated and largely unaccepted man.

One of those protégés was rancher Maurice Wright, who authored a book, *The Jeffery Method of Horse Handling** and a videotape with the same title.

An essential part of Jeffery's method was to advance and then retreat while working with a green horse. Why? It is against human nature to retreat, but to reassure the horse we must learn to do just that. Horses are intimidated by unfamiliar objects moving toward them. Approach a green horse dragging a tarpaulin. What happens? Panic! What does it inspire? Flight!

On the other hand, drag the tarp *away* from the green horse. What happens? Reassurance. A retreating object is not behaving in a predatory

---

* Maurice Wright, *The Jeffery Method of Horse Handling*, Dyamberin, Armidale, 1973

manner. It is not threatening. It provokes curiosity. Soon, the horse will be following the tarp, smelling it, investigating it.

Green colts on cattle drives, if placed in the drag (the rear of the herd), will develop confidence as the cattle move away from them. A green colt in the drag will, at the end of a long cattle drive, have developed confidence to drive and pursue cattle. It will be reining well from being

Fear of the ball. It is a novel stimulus and therefore a possible predator.

Same reaction as in the first photo, fear!

Ball rolls away from colt. A non-predatory retreat.

Colt soon has the confidence to smell the ball.

Now the colt begins to push the ball.

The fear is gone and Pat Parelli now can place the ball on the colt's back.

Completely desentized to what it feared was a predator, the colt now allows the ball to be bounced off his back.

constantly turned this way and that to encourage stragglers in the herd to keep up. Most working cowboys are not sophisticated horsemen, but the work they do—herding and driving cattle, and opening and closing gates—produces good working horses.

Because we are a reasoning species, and a predatory species, we tend to regard the horse as a stupid animal because of its flightiness. The horse, however, has existed far longer on this planet than has man. Its flight response to *anything* that suggests predation is not stupidity. It is nature's wisdom.

In his book, *Evolutionary Psychology,** Dylen Evans points out that false alarms are less costly to a prey animal than is slow detection. Horses who are slow to detect danger in the wild do not survive to reproduce. "Therefore," Evans states, "we should expect the predator detection module to be fast and inaccurate, rather than slow and precise." It is speed and inaccuracy in flight response that cause most of the serious behavior problems we have with horses, such as shying, running away, bolting,

---

* Dylen Evans, *Evolutionary Psychology*, Icon Books, Ltd., Cambridge, U.K., 1999

bucking, and pulling back when tied. Yet, it is this very flightiness that has made the horse so useful to us, because we can channel that flight instinct down the racetrack, over fences, into the collar, after the cow, around the barrels, and up the mountain.

It is *so* important to understand the horse's reaction to predatory behavior because it is the essence of what makes natural horsemanship work. Note that *all* of the effective clinicians involved in this revolution can, on one hand, be so gentle, so soft, so reassuring to the horse. Yet, as required, they can be *so* assertive. This is why so many of their students cannot get the same results as their teachers. Some—typically younger men—cannot become soft enough, passive enough, gentle enough to completely reassure the horse. Others—typically women—cannot assume an assertive enough attitude, expression, and stance when that is needed.

Because the whirl of a rope, the flutter of a plastic flag, or the raising of a stick is a predatory threat to the horse, its response is to move *away*. We reinforce the response by removing the threatening stimulus. The movement of the horse—which may be only a step forward or backward, a momentary disengagement of the hindquarter, or a lateral move—produces capitulation in the horse. It elevates the handler's dominance status. It increases the horse's desire to follow what it perceives to be a lead horse.

This is why clinicians drill their students on their body language, which includes their posture, where they focus their gaze, the expressions on their faces, which way their toes point, whether their chins are up or down, and what their hands are saying. The horse sees it all and reacts accordingly.

I once had an extraordinary experience in Africa. It was dawn, and the hippopotami that had been grazing all night had retired to the Mara River. One hungry, half-grown hippo had remained behind to graze a while longer. As I videotaped it, I saw two male lions stalking it, one from the front and one from the rear. When the lion in front was close enough for a charge he launched himself toward the young hippo, which raised its head. As soon as it realized death was approaching, it opened its huge mouth, bellowed, and charged headfirst at the oncoming lion. The *predator* slid to a stop, whirled, and fled, pursued by the *prey*. The other lion simply abandoned its stalk.

A prey creature survived by displaying *predatory behavior*.

CHAPTER FIVE

Tools

Zoologically speaking, we are one of the larger primates. Perhaps we can be described as a primate that is endowed with a remarkable brain, walks erect, has an opposable thumb, is a hunting and gathering species, and is an extensive tool user.

Now quite a few other species, ranging from chimpanzees to certain birds, are also tool users, but sticking twigs into holes to capture ants is a long way from operating a computer, let alone *inventing* one. The bow and arrow is an incredibly complex tool when one considers how long we just used knives, spears, and axes made of stone before we started using the bow and arrow. The use of tools is in our DNA. We can't resist them. Got a problem? Buy a tool! "Only $19.99, but wait! Order now and we'll send you *another* one, *FREE!*"

It has taken us about six thousand years to figure out the best way to communicate with horses, and even now that we have learned we still want to do it with tools, especially tools that can cause pain. Go to any horse exposition and watch what is the most common purchase made at the trade show. It's the *whip*! So many shoppers, carrying new whips, and they *love* horses.

The whip *is* a legitimate tool. It serves as an extension of the human arm and helps us to communicate with the horse. It isn't supposed to be used to flog a horse, to inflict pain, or to obtain acquiescence via coercion.

That's why the natural horsemanship clinicians don't use the word "whip." The word has an ugly connotation because it is so often misused. They call them "sticks," "flags," "sticks with a string attached," "ropes," "riatas," or "lines." And, they don't "whip" (the verb) horses with them, because there is no need to do so. Their goal is a response to *small* signals. Lightness! They *signal* with their non-whips.

The spur is another legitimate tool. It can be used to create a greater pressure stimulus than can be obtained with the leg alone. It facilitates lateral movement in the horse. It shouldn't and needn't be used to puncture the horse or to inflict unnecessary pain.

In 1958 I went to the Coliseum in Los Angeles to watch a group of well-known *charros* perform. These Mexican horsemen were superb riders, and I admired the classical dressage movements they were able to inspire in their horses. Afterward, I went to the arena area below to see the horses. All of them were bleeding from wounds inflicted by the big, sharp, roweled spurs the riders wore. Totally unnecessary!

At the Wolf Creek Ranch near Grass Valley, California, a man named Eitan performs what he calls "cowboy dressage," doing all of the classical maneuvers the charros performed, but he does it with dull spurs, on a loose rein, and his performance is better than that of the charros.

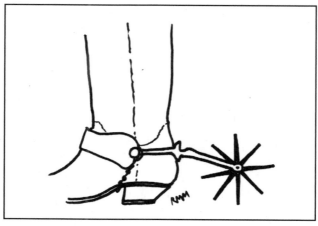

An early Hawaiian spur of Mexican/Spanish style. The dangling "jingle bobs" make a ringing sound. An old retired cowboy recalled, "We like it, you know...I guess they keep everybody happy." Including the horse?

An early California vaquero spur. Is such a spur justifiable? Why do modern horse trainers not use such spurs?

AN OLD SPUR FOUND IN CALIFORNIA'S SAN EMIDEO HILLS

"The ancient Moorish spur with its over-all length of ten inches, two-inch wrought iron band and six-inch rowels had been well-worn long before it had been lost or left in the San Emideo Hills. But the fine filigree workmanship of the Moslem crescents was still discernable in all its details despite the rust of years. Its delicately tapered rowels come to a fine point and with its triple rowel locks, it still had the appearance of being a brutal and indispensable item in the equipment of some far-ranging horseman of this country's early history."

— *From These Were the Vaqueros* (1974) by Arnold Rojas, horseman, vaquero, historian, and author. I was privileged to know him.

Alfonso Aguilar, a charro from Patzcuaro, Mexico, is today a natural horsemanship clinician. He demonstrates dressage and reining maneuvers from his horses sans bridle or saddle. His horses are so responsive that he doesn't need spurs or even a bridle.

**ON MOORISH HORSEMANSHIP
"TRAINING A HORSE"**

"The Arabs esteem their horses beyond measure of price, treat them with tenderness, and cherish them as a rite and part of their faith, even as a member of their family. They are trained with much patience and care until the time comes to teach them to fear the spur more than anything in this world, animate or inanimate. This schooling is fraught with so much pain and severity that ever after, at the urge of the spur the horse will throw himself against any living creature or even a stone wall, or in whatever way his master guides.

The vaquero followed this practice on his mustang and it can be easily understood why old *lazadores* could force a horse, against his instinct and near panic, up to a grizzly bear and rope the lord of the North American wilds and truss him up like a pig, and why *golpe de caballo* (blow with a horse) was so potent a weapon. It was used by Californians to force their mounts against their opponents and knock them down with the force of the blow."

—Arnold Rojas, *These Were the Vaqueros*

Go into any saddlery, or look in any equestrian catalog at the bit section. What you will see is a collection of tools that look like a display of Medieval torture devices. The advertisements accompanying these bits often assert that they have special effects you need for the hard-to-stop horse, the horse that refuses to flex, the hard-mouthed horse, the stiff-necked horse, and the cold-jawed horse. There are "correctional" bits, "gag" bits, and so on.

How can we reconcile the immense variety and purported effects of these bits when nearly all of the clinicians responsible for the revolution in horsemanship start colts in a simple halter? They don't move them to the bit until the colt is completely responsive to the halter, backing, turning, even spinning. They have the colts doing rollbacks, flexing, and stopping properly. Then, when the bit is introduced, they use a simple iron snaffle bit devoid of gimmicks, gadgets, bells, and whistles. Doesn't this *prove* that control of the horse does not and should not depend upon a severe bit? Observe that these clinicians will, when presented with problem horses— outlaws, spoiled brats, horses Monty Roberts diplomatically calls "remedial horses" (our prisons are filled with "remedial convicts") invariably reform them through: a) reschooling them on the ground, usually in a simple halter, and b) riding them in a halter or a simple snaffle bit.

They can obtain the desired results with these techniques because:

1) The horse is a fast learner. Flight animals must be fast learners or they do not survive.

2) Fast learners can quickly be *counter conditioned*. This process establishes an acceptable response to a stimulus as a replacement for an unacceptable response. For example, a head-shy horse can quickly learn to allow its head to be handled using counter conditioning. The technique extinguishes an habitual, undesirable response by eliciting a simultaneous distracting stimulus.

3) Fast learners can quickly be conditioned to consistently respond to a given stimulus. Conditioning or the establishment of a conditioned response is the process by which an individual learns to respond in a consistent manner to a specific stimulus.

Most horse training consists of the establishment of conditioned responses. Skillful trainers can do this with remarkable speed, so fast, in fact, that to the uninitiated what is accomplished seems magical. In the past, great horsemen were often accused of witchcraft because what they could do with a horse seemed inexplicable to the average person. Even today the casual observer often decides that "hypnotism" or some mystical talent possessed by the clinician is the only possible explanation for the swift and dramatic changes that occur in the public clinics and demonstrations that are so popular today. Or, the skeptical insist that the clinician had "worked with that horse before" or "slipped him a drug." In fact, as I have tried to explain in this book, everything that occurs in natural horsemanship is scientifically based and quite predictable. *Anybody* can be taught to do this if they have sufficient desire, but of course not everybody will do it equally well because of variations in our coordination, physical responses, experience, confidence, and awareness.

The Traditional California Method

Elsewhere in this book I praise the traditional California method of horsemanship, which evolved in colonial California, persisted well into the twentieth century, and now exists only in superficial remnants. It is still taught by a few clinicians such as Mike Bridges of Halfway, Oregon, Peter Campbell of Wheatland, Wyoming, and a few others. I also admit that

some aspects of the traditional California vaquero (anglicized to "buckaroo") method were still unnecessarily coercive, as described by such writers as Ortega and Connell.*

A spade bit.

* *California Stock Horse* by Luis B Ortega, 1949, News Publishing Co., Sacramento, CA; *Hackamore Reinsman* by Ed Connell, 1952, The Longhorn Press, Cisco, TX.

This painting by cowboy artist Ernie Morris depicts classical Californios. The young horse on the left is in the hackamore. Note the tapa ojos blindfold. The horse on the right, in the spade bit, is a finished bridle horse as indicated by the tuft of mane at the withers.

Ed Connell recorded for posterity the methods of the Californios— the California vaqueros. His books, *Reinsman of the West—Bridles and Bits* and *Hackamore Reinsman*, are classics, available today from Lennoche Publishers of Wimberly, Texas. More recently Lennoche has published *Vaquero Style Horsemanship*, a compilation of articles and letters by and about Ed Connell.

The horsemanship that evolved in colonial California, originating in Morocco and migrating to Spain and then to Mexico, led to the most sophisticated form of native horsemanship the world has ever known. Yet it included elements of harshness that today's natural horsemanship clinicians have eliminated completely. *Vaquero Style Horsemanship*, especially, describes forceful methods, which were deemed necessary and traditional in the past, but which have been replaced by psychological methods that work more rapidly, more safely, and even more effectively.

The very best clinicians have combined the California vaquero method with classical European horsemanship to achieve the incredible results seen today.

In the California method, colts were started in a hackamore and then slowly and progressively moved into the spade bit. To the uninformed, the spade bit looks like a torture device. It isn't, and it is appropriate here to explain why it is not, and to rationalize its use.

The colt is started in a *hackamore*. This word is an anglicized corruption of the Spanish word *jaquima. La jaquima* means "the halter." A hackamore is simply a halter. The nosepiece, however, called a *bosal*, is initially heavy and made of carefully braided and shaped rawhide. It is freely suspended from the poll by a thin leather "hanger." To keep it from slipping over the poll, a rope *fiador* (anglicized to "Theodore") is fastened around the throatlatch. The heavy bosal encourages flexion at the poll because that position is most comfortable to the horse. A *mecaté* (which means "rope" in Spanish and has been anglicized to "McCarty" or "McCarthy") is wrapped around the bosal, below the jaw, and serves as reins. Its long tail serves as a lead rope.

All initial training on the ground, and in the saddle, is done in the hackamore. Thus far please note the similarity between the traditional California method and the method almost all leading clinicians use to start colts. The only difference is in the design of the halter: a *jaquima*, rope halter, or ordinary flat halter.

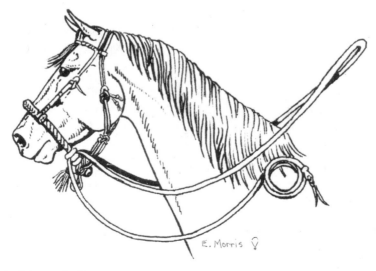

The hackamore, by Ernie Morris.

THE SPADE BIT

"The spade [bit] was old in Africa centuries before Father Kino ever set eyes toward California. And, one can find pictures of modern day Ethiopians mounted on mules wearing ring bits identical with the *'Chilena'* bit."

—Arnold Rojas, *These Were the Vaqueros*

The traditional California horse was worked in the hackamore for a long time, one or more years, and kept in it until very well trained. The young horse's mouth was "unspoiled," undamaged, and sensitive. Then a leverage bit, most commonly a spade bit, was placed into its mouth without reins, and the horse was further ridden in the hackamore. Eventually reins were attached to the leverage bit, but were not used initially. Later, and very gradually, the reins were used in conjunction with the hackamore reins. A good hackamore reinsman never caused the horse to fight the

A young horse in the classical California two rein. Still in a hackamore with a light bosal, but now carrying a spade bit to which he gradually makes a transition.

bit, elevate its nose, or gape its mouth. Progressively lighter and lighter bosals were used, and very gradually the reins connected to the leverage bit became the primary signaling device. All of this took a lot of time. Ultimately the hackamore reins were discarded and the result was the finished bridle horse—the classical California reined cowhorse—superbly agile, so responsive, and so *light*.

The Natural Horsemanship Method

The revolution in horsemanship features a method *similar to* but not identical to the traditional California method we have just described. It is different because of the founding fathers of the revolution—men like Tom Dorrance and Ray Hunt and those who followed them, emulated them, became clinicians, and started a revolution in the ancient art and science of horsemanship.

Although these clinicians advocate starting horses in a halter (*la jaquima*), they soon switch to a snaffle bit. The snaffle bit was never a part of the original California method. Keep in mind that the earliest clinicians

This is Walter Wisdom, foreman on a ranch I worked on in 1951 in Colorado. He is riding BigShot, a colt he started in a leverage bit. He did a great job. "It doesn't matter what you start them in," he claimed. "It's how you use the equipment."

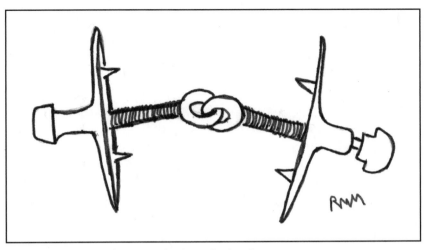

An ancient Egyptian bit. Note the sharp cheek spikes.

came out of the Pacific *Northwest*, not the *Southwest*. They all came out of Northern California, Oregon, Idaho, and Montana. The Dorrance family emigrated from Canada to Oregon. Early in the twentieth century Bill Dorrance went to California, where he observed vaquero horsemanship and then brought it home to his brothers, including Tom.

Tom, the brilliant, sensitive pacifist, adopted the concept, but utilized the snaffle bit. The snaffle came to the New World via England. It did not become part of the California method until the early twentieth century.

> "If you start a colt with a snaffle bit, no matter how careful you are in the early stages of his training, you are bound to put pressure on those tender bars at some time. With the hackamore this cannot happen."
>
> — Luis B. Ortega, *California Stock Horse* (1940)

When I attended my first Ray Hunt clinic, I was surprised to see the vaquero's mecaté, adapted to a snaffle bit. A hybrid form of horsemanship had been born, incorporating the vaquero's starting method taken to an even gentler extreme. The heavy and uncomfortable bosal had been replaced by a thin rope halter. Then, a transfer was made, not to the vaquero's leverage spade bit, but to a simple snaffle bit.

Lo! The least coercive, gentlest, most humane form of horsemanship the world had ever seen was born. Thanks to the fact that the right historical moment had occurred, a revolution in horsemanship ensued.

Tools are an essential part of horsemanship. The choice of the tools is the option of the particular clinician and of the clinician's student. It doesn't matter whether the colt is initially trained in an ordinary halter, Monty Roberts' Dually Halter, Steve Edwards' rope "Come Along," Ray Hunt's Cowboy Rope Halter, an old-time rope Johnson halter, or a traditional Spanish hackamore. The important thing is that the mouth isn't hurt early on in the training, and that the horse is well trained to lead, to stand tied, to turn, to follow, to back up, to disengage its hindquarters, and to move laterally. All of this can be taught with nothing in the mouth, while simultaneously a trusting bond develops between horse and horseman. It isn't necessary to have anything in the mouth while a horse learns to accept a saddle, grooming, having its feet handled, and to accept all sorts of ordinarily frightening stimuli. What is important *is* that the halter, whatever its form, be used skillfully, humanely, and wisely.

It doesn't matter whether the bit is some form of snaffle, or some form of leverage bit. What *does* matter is the skill with which the bit is

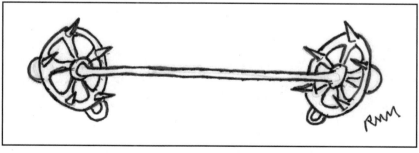

This Hyksos bit, circa 1800 BC, typifies the natural human assumption that it is necessary to inflict pain in order to control the horse. Note the cruel spikes on the sides of the bit. There was no understanding that conditioned response could be established in the horse quickly and easily, with very gentle training methods we today call "natural horsemanship."

used, that it not be introduced prematurely, that the transference from halter to bit is made with the greatest skill and precision, and that the bit should never be regarded or used as an instrument of torture or to punish a horse. It is a signaling device. It isn't used to *force* a horse to turn or stop. It is to signal a horse already trained to turn or stop. Yes, weapons are tools, but a bit should only be a tool, never a weapon.

I don't believe I have ever heard a clinician condemn a curb bit. But, most of them teach the use of the snaffle because a) the student may not have the expertise or the emotional control to use a curb bit properly, and b) they want the student to understand that the bit is not a weapon but a tool, a signaling device. Both snaffles and curb bits can be used abusively but it is much easier to inflict damage with the curb bit.

Hobbles

I briefly discussed hobbles earlier and mentioned the profound psychological effect various kinds of hobbles have on the horse in that they inhibit flight. Anything that inhibits flight will induce submissiveness in the horse. Hobbles are defined as any device that restrains the legs and inhibits movement.

Argentine rawhide hobbles.

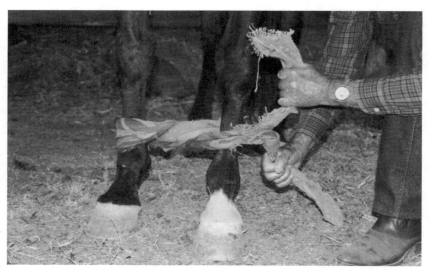

Applying a gunny sack hobble. The safest kind of training hobble I have fond for a first experience. Then I switch to leather hobbles.

It is interesting that, while today's recreational rider often has an excessive dependency on and respect for such tools as bits, spurs, and whips, they usually regard hobbles as an unnecessary and cruel device. Perhaps hobbles suggest handcuffs to the novice horseman, a punishing contraption for criminals and violent felons. Many riders assume that hobbles are only for horses used on pack trips so they can graze on mountain pastures, or for working cow horses that are left unattended on open plains.

These uses are correct, of course, but I believe that *all* domestic horses should be trained to hobbles and that proper hobble training is an integral part of natural horsemanship. A trained horse should accept complete and prolonged physical restraint of all four legs, separately, one at a time, any two at a time, any three at a time, or all four at a time.

It is not my intent here to teach the various methods of hobbling, but rather to explain its rationale, extol its value, and justify its use. I even advocate that the newborn foal be taught that any or all of its legs can be controlled and immobilized. This is a vital part of my foal-training program. Regardless of the age at which a horse is "broke to hobbles" or "hobble broke," it will never forget this lesson. It lasts a lifetime.

Why hobbles?

1. The properly hobble-broke horse is less likely to panic and injure itself if its legs are ever entangled in wire, rope, or fencing.

2. As I have repeatedly stated (because it is so vital a concept), control of the limbs will cause subordination in the horse, and it does this without training of any kind. Simply restraining leg use will cause horses to signal submission and behave submissively to the handler. This was all that John Rarey, the most esteemed of the nineteenth-century American horse tamers, did to alter his subjects' attitudes. He demonstrated his Rarey leg strap internationally, and called his method "*Rareyfication.*"

3. The quickest and simplest way to stop certain unwanted behaviors in horses is to hobble them, provided they have been well trained to hobbles. For example, some horses persistently begin to move off whenever an attempt is made to mount them. Although there are several ways to stop this behavior, one of the simplest is to hobble the forelimbs and then repeatedly mount and dismount from both sides. Another example is pawing in the stall, in a horse trailer when it stops moving, or at feeding time. A hobbled horse cannot paw.

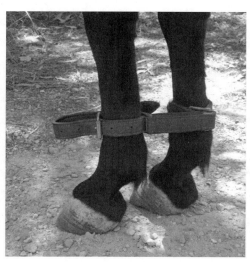

Leather hobbles.

Certain techniques used by the clinicians may not be technically considered hobbling, but since they involve restraint of the legs and have the same psychological effects, I will discuss them here. In fact, these techniques are good precursors to the actual application of hobbles because once the horse accepts them it will be much less likely to resist actual hobbles.

Ray Hunt often ropes one hind foot of the green horse he is working with from horseback, then patiently and persistently plays with it. Initially the green horse may kick and jerk the leg bearing the noose, but eventually it will quietly submit and allow the foot to be drawn upward off the ground. It is a lesson in yielding and in flight control.

Pat Parelli can be seen putting the loop of a lariat around the pastern of a foreleg. The horse is saddled while Pat is on the ground. He then takes a dally around the saddle horn and pulls the rope taut for a moment, elevating the leg. It is then released promptly. This is done repeatedly until the horse yields the leg without panic, and will allow it to be suspended for a long time. Once this is learned it is a simple matter to apply a Rarey-type leg strap, or just wrap eight or ten feet of soft cotton rope around the flexed leg to restrain it. The horse will have learned to accept the hobbling of one leg with its attendant benefits.

An Australian hobble, used above the knees of the horse's forelimb. Many areas of the Outback are treeless and stock horses are hobbled and left loose while the rider eats.

CHAPTER SIX

Desensitization

Only a dozen large mammals have been successfully domesticated by man, and there are several reasons the horse was one of those suitable. Obviously its speed, size, and strength were important attributes. Additionally, the horse is a gregarious herd creature that feels safest when it is well led, and the human, serving as a surrogate herd leader, can fulfill a lot of the horse's needs. The speed with which horses learn, their incredible memory, and their sensory awareness also facilitated domestication.

More than anything else, however, the horse's ability to become quickly desensitized to frightening stimuli made it the most valuable of domestic animals. Were it not for that characteristic, how would we have been able to use horses so extensively in warfare, for the herding of livestock, for hunting, for pulling and hauling all sorts of things, and for high speed transportation?

Newly captured* wild horses can, in a matter of hours, be gentled and taught to accept and respond to a rider, using methods shared by the various clinicians teaching natural horsemanship. What other animal, born in the wild and having spent its life there, could so quickly be tamed and domesticated? Bryan Neubert, Dennis Reis, Richard Shrake, Pat

---

* We use the common term "wild" horses, realizing the American mustang, like Australia's brumbies and so many other so-called "wild" horses are actually *feral* horses, a domestic species born and surviving in a natural environment free from contact with humans.

The speed of learning and of desensitization in the horse is demonstrated in this series of photographs taken over a 3 hour period. Dave Dohnel, owner of Frontier Pack Train, starts a recently adopted BLM mustang colt, captured in the wild. He routinely uses these horses to carry his customers up into the high mountains around Bishop, California.

After round-penning the colt until it joins up with him, he rubs it all over its body for an hour. Then he cautiously mounts it.

The colt has learned that this human will not harm him and is a leader to be trusted. Here Dave teaches the colt lateral flexion of the head and neck.

Another hour has gone by. He has introduced the colt to the snaffle bit and bridle and is now desensitizing it to a saddle pad and blanket.

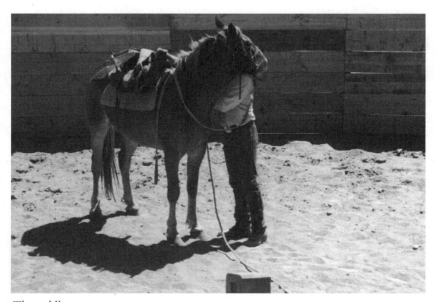

The saddle comes next.

But when girthed and turned loose, the colt bucks violently.

...only to return to Dave for reassurance and to follow him.

Dave now mounts the saddled colt...

...and uneventfully rides him in a halter.
Afterward, Dave's daughter rode the colt from time to time, as well as Dave. The next spring, one year after these photographs were taken, Dave led another pack trip up into the mustang country riding his colt, now named Keno. He rode him in a halter.

Parelli, Monty Roberts, and Clinton Anderson all have made commercial videos demonstrating the starting of captured wild mustangs. From the introduction of the trainer to a rideable horse takes, in each case, about three hours, and it is done without violence.

A major obstacle in starting tame colts, let alone wild colts, is overcoming their instinctive flight reactions to frightening sensory stimuli. This can, with appropriate skill, be done so rapidly that it is amazing how many supposedly gentle, well trained, and even older horses are afraid of ordinary harmless things. These include water hoses, electric clippers, horse trailers, bicycles, umbrellas, motorcycles, balloons, flags, farriers, veterinarians, men in general, ropes, plastic, paper, and all kinds of other animals.

A technique routinely used in breaking colts with traditional cowboy horsemanship is "sacking out." In this method, a halter-broke, but unridden, colt is repeatedly stroked with a flapping sack or blanket. At first terrified, the colt soon learns the stimulus (which is visual, auditory, *and* tactile) will not harm it, and eventually becomes indifferent to it.

Technically this process is known as "flooding," wherein the brain is bombarded with stimuli until habituation occurs. Habituation is a process wherein an individual is exposed to a repeated stimulus, with no reinforcement of any kind, until there is no response. Thereafter, the colt is, in effect, desensitized to the stimulus and therefore is gentler and safer to handle.

Flooding unquestionably works. The problem is that it is potentially dangerous. An unexpected or violent reaction could easily result in injury to horse or to human. So, except when desensitizing newborn foals, we do not recommend flooding as a preferred technique to desensitize horses for the average horse owner.

Although it is much slower than flooding, a safer technique is to progressively desensitize the horse by using the advance-and-retreat method described earlier, or even the pursuit of an unfamiliar and frightening object also described earlier. A horse can follow a tarp being dragged *away* from it until confidence and curiosity develop and fear dissipates.

In any case, exposure to a great variety of sights, sounds, smells, and tactile experiences is necessary to produce a horse that is as free of fearful flight reactions as possible. Realizing the horse cannot reason and accept a white blanket if it was desensitized with a black blanket, or a hissing insecticide bomb if it was desensitized to a liquid sprayer, the more varied and intense the stimuli are, the better the results will be. As long as it does not cause pain, horses can be desensitized to *any* sensory stimulus. This desensitization can include flags and flares, explosions and gunfire, bells and whistles, pigs and pythons.

Another example of progressive desensitization is useful when riding and the horse shies. It may shy at a suspicious object on or beside the trail, at a ditch or stream, or even at a puddle that must be crossed. Rather than spurring and whipping at the horse's reluctance, one can calmly ride *past* it, at some distance. Then, turn the horse *toward* the frightening object, and ride past it again and again. Gradually, the fear will lessen and each pass can be closer to the cause. Eventually, the horse will become curious as the fear subsides, and will probably want to smell and investigate the object causing the problem.

What has happened? By riding *past* the object instead of *toward* it, the object seems to go *away* from the horse. Predators don't move away. Additionally, with each pass, the horse sees the object with a different eye. Because horses' eyes are not in the front of their heads, as ours are, they do not have our binocular stereoscopic vision, which gives us excellent depth perception. Instead, their eyes are placed laterally on the sides of their head. This is an advantage to a prey animal who must see all around himself in order to stay alive, but it means each eye sends a separate image to the brain. Not only does this impede depth perception, but it also means a horse may be desensitized to something with one eye but not necessarily with the other eye. That's why repeatedly riding past a frightening thing, turning toward it again and again, quells the horse's fear.

Another useful technique with the shying horse is to make whatever it fears become *the best place in the world*. How? By making it a resting place once the fear has been conquered. You see, endlessly going back and forth past the object is *work*. Once the fear is gone, and the curiosity that replaces the fear is satisfied, *boredom* sets in. After several rests near the previously frightening object, the horse will think that's the best place to be. Isn't this more sensible, more preferable than whipping and spurring and hurting the horse? The *reason* he's afraid is because he doesn't want to get hurt.

There is a reason horses can be more quickly habituated or desensitized to startling stimuli than any other domestic animal. It is because the horse *is* a flight creature and if, in nature, it could not quickly desensitize to frightening but harmless stimuli, it would never stop running. There would be no time for wild horses to rest, eat, drink, or reproduce. That's because, in the wild, prey creatures are constantly and incessantly alarmed by any sudden and unfamiliar stimulus.

It is interesting that some of the horse's related species are less flighty than the horse.

Specifically, the ass is less flighty. It evolved in steep, arid terrain. Blind flight, so effective for the plains-dwelling horse, could be fatal here. Donkeys, therefore, make decisions rather than blindly fleeing. They may choose to flee, or to stay put because they feel safe (hence, the reputation for "stubbornness"), or to attack (hence, their value in guarding sheep against predators such as coyotes). But, they are more challenging to train. With horses, we simply control and direct the overwhelming flight response. The ass makes its own decisions. The same is usually true of the hybrid offspring of the horse and donkey, the mule.

Zebra, when threatened, rather than fleeing, will often mill around, their striped patterns melding and presenting a confusing image to the predator. Zebra, again, are extremely difficult to train and have never been truly domesticated. It is a myth, however, that they cannot be broken to ride.

CHAPTER SEVEN

Understanding Reinforcement

We understand that some behavior is genetically predetermined. It is instinctive. Other behaviors are learned. An example familiar to us in dogs is that they mark their territories with urine. That is instinctive. However, we can teach the dog not to do that in the house. That is learned behavior.

Some learned behaviors are achieved instantly, without repetition or reinforcement. The imprinting phenomenon in the newborn prey animal is an example of immediate learning. Certain traumatic experiences can, with a single occurrence, produce a lasting phobia.

However, most learned behaviors are the result of *reinforcement*. Reinforcement is a reward that is given consistently after a behavior occurs until the behavior becomes a conditioned response. There are two kinds of reinforcement: negative reinforcement and positive reinforcement. Confusion exists concerning an understanding of these two entities.

Many people think that "negative" reinforcement means "punishment," whereas "positive" reinforcement means "reward." This is incorrect. *Both* positive and negative reinforcement are rewards. In fact, most horse training involves the use of negative reinforcement more than the use of positive reinforcement. Many traditional horse trainers use negative reinforcement exclusively and get very good results. That's because negative reinforcement is a reward.

Negative Reinforcement

In negative reinforcement we reward the horse by removing discomfort when we get desired behavior. Examples:

- We pressure a horse to move forward. When he moves forward, we reward him by removing the pressure.

- We pressure a horse to move laterally. When he does so, we remove the pressure.

- We pressure a horse to back up. When he backs up, we reward him by removing the pressure.

The reward is *comfort*. We remove pressure. That's negative reinforcement, and it is the reward system we primarily use to fix behavioral responses in horses.

Positive Reinforcement

Here, too, the reward is comfort, but instead of achieving it by removing discomfort, we simply *add comfort* when we observe a desired behavior, rather than *removing discomfort*. What kind of comfort can be used as a reward? Well, there are relatively few in life, but they are all the things that make us feel good. Examples:

- Rest if we are tired.

- A drink if we are thirsty.

- Air if we are winded.

- Cold if we are too warm.

- Warmth if we feel cold.

- Food if we are hungry, or, in the case of horses, palatable food *anytime* because horses by nature spend most of their day eating.

- Company is a reward if we are lonely, and horses are group creatures.

- Praise, petting, and stroking the horse are rewards because horses crave acceptance.

- In humans, powerful rewards include sex, money, trophies, medals, and titles, but horses are above these sort of things.

Some horse trainers use positive reinforcement almost exclusively, using food rewards or linking food rewards to a signal, such as in clicker training, which is widely used in the training of other species, such as dogs, primates, and sea mammals. In fact, clicker training is now being used to enhance the performance of juvenile human athletes. Food rewards, the clicker signal, and a visual target have been linked in what is called target training. Clicker and target training were described in our previous book, *The Revolution in Horsemanship*.

Traditionally, most horse trainers spurn the use of food rewards to positively reinforce desired behaviors. They believe that it spoils horses, makes them "mouthy," and encourages biting and disrespect. Yet, some

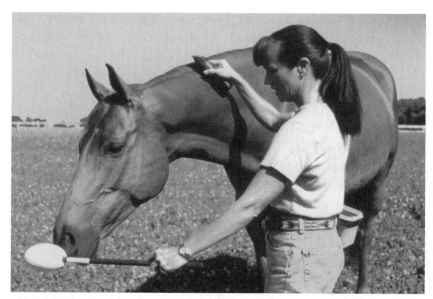

Shawna Karrasch, formerly a dolphin trainer, uses reinforcement (food treats) and a target and clicks to do her "target training." Here she does it to train a horse at liberty to accept electric clippers.

of the best trainers in the world use food as rewards extensively, including many of the best circus and trick horse trainers and the best classical horse trainers in the world, such as those in Vienna's Spanish Riding School.

What this tells us is that the use of food rewards, as with any other training method, requires expertise and experience. If a method works well for one person, but not for another person, *one* of them is doing it wrong. A trainer's ineptness with any given method does *not* necessarily mean the method is wrong.

When using rewards to positively reinforce desired behaviors, there are several rules.

1.   The reward must *immediately* follow the desired behavior. A human may be reinforced by a delayed reward ("Good job, you'll get a bonus next month"), but a horse needs the reward right now. So, a spectacular lead change may be rewarded by a minute of rest or, a great stop may be rewarded by immediately dismounting and loosening the girth. Or, a good maneuver may be rewarded by softly stroking the neck several times and perhaps an audible signal such as "Good boy." Or, coming to us on command and willingly putting the head into the halter may be rewarded by a food treat. In any case, the reward should come as soon after the desired behavior as possible, a concept known as *immediacy*.

2.   The reward should be *brief*: a slice of carrot, a pinch of grain. Do not reward the horse with a whole carrot or a big handful of grain. A brief stroking, not prolonged petting, will do, as will a minute of rest, not an hour. Why brief? Because if too prolonged, the *reason* for the reward may be forgotten. Small, immediate rewards are more effective in fixing behavior than are large delayed rewards.

Reinforcement in Natural Horsemanship

The gurus of natural horsemanship use *both* positive and negative reinforcement, and they use it skillfully. For example, say the horse is being taught to back up. First, discomfort is caused by creating pressure. As soon as the horse backs, the pressure is immediately removed. This is negative reinforcement. We have replaced discomfort with comfort. Then, we further reward the horse by adding new comfort. When backing while astride, the reward might be to softly stroke the neck and say, "Good boy." If backing from the ground, we can add comfort by just assuming a relaxed posture, smiling, and saying, "Good boy."

Once a behavior, established by means of positive reinforcement, is fully conditioned rewards may be given inconsistently. In other words, the reward being used for positive reinforcement is not provided every time the desired response is obtained. Instead, it is given unpredictably. This *variable* or *intermittent* reward schedule will actually enhance the response.

As an example, suppose we use a food treat to reward a horse for coming to us in response to the command "Come!" After the horse consistently comes to us, indicating a conditioned response, then we may skip the reward now and then, or perhaps substitute a stroke or two, or praise. Mix it up. This seems to increase anticipation of a possible reward, and accelerate the response.

Remember that the goal in our relationship with a horse is 100 percent trust and respect, but zero percent fear. Then the horse wants to be close to us because it feels safest near us. It wants to please us and have our approval because it wants acceptance, especially from us the herd leader.

CHAPTER EIGHT

Feel

Ray Hunt was the man who launched this revolution in the late 1970s. We must acknowledge that his mentor, his "teacher" as he reverently referred to him, was Tom Dorrance. Tom, author of the book *True Unity** with Milly Hunt Porter, spoke of "feel." His brother, Bill Dorrance, also a major contributing instigator of the revolution, also spoke of "feel." Ray Hunt also proclaimed "feel" as a major factor in this progressive form of horsemanship that we have labeled "natural." Yet, they never defined "feel." With some trepidation, may we offer an involved explanation of what we think "feel" comprises in regard to the relationship between horse and human?

"Feel" from the Human Standpoint

On the human side, "feel" is the ability to detect the response of the horse and to anticipate its consequences. The ability to do this depends upon certain qualities, which will vary from person to person. These are the qualities:

1. **Experience**. "Experience" means that no person, regardless of how willing he or she is to learn, and regardless of how well endowed

---

* Tom Dorrance and Milly Hunt Porter, *True Unity*, Give-It-A-Go Enterprises, Tuscarora, Nevada, 1987

with the attributes which follow, can master natural horsemanship without extensive experience with great numbers of horses.

2. **Awareness**. This varies from one individual to another. Our senses vary in acuity and our reaction times vary with our neurological makeup and our physiology. Hand-eye coordination is inborn. Although training can improve it, the highest level is still limited in us genetically.

3. **Training**. Although some people are by nature more suitable to becoming proficient horsemen, no one is wise enough to know it all. It would take more than one lifetime. All exceptional horsemen have learned from others, and today we are fortunate that modern communications and the revolution in horsemanship have made it possible for every aspirant to become proficient at a reasonably early age. Examples abound. Pat Parelli was well on his way in his twenties, thanks to the influence of *his* teachers. More recently, Clinton Anderson has become an important clinician before the age of thirty thanks to the influence of his teachers, who included Pat Parelli. The more we learn, the more we can pass on to the next generation. The horse will be the greatest beneficiary, along with the humans who work with horses.

4. **Desire**. Traditional horsemanship and natural horsemanship as well are complex subjects. They involve athletic physical prowess, intelligence to comprehend and apply the intricate methods involved and, above all, emotional stability. The horse, a flighty creature, is highly and adversely responsive to three very common human emotions: fear, impatience, and anger. This extremely perceptive species can detect these emotions in a human handler even if the human does everything possible to conceal them. They then evoke confusion, intimidation, apprehension, and fear in the horse. These, in turn cause a desire to preferably *flee*, or, alternatively, to *fight*. Therefore, the aspiring natural horseman must be able to contain these emotions or, at least, when they arise, to abandon working with the horse and *leave* until once

again emotionally stable. No more important advice can be given to the aspiring horseman than to *quit* when emotions arise. Of course, ideally, we never become emotional, but we all vary in our reactions and responses, and some of us are more volatile than others. For such people, the best course is to *stop* when we feel impatient or angry or frustrated.

FRANCISCO ZAMORA

When the great Mexican horseman Francisco Zamora was in his early twenties I saw him perform at our county fair. I was so impressed with his horsemanship that I went up afterwards to talk with him. As we conversed a man about Francisco's own age knelt nearby wrapping up equipment. He was Zamora's hired hand.

"From whom did you learn your horsemanship?" I asked, after complimenting him on his memorable performance.

"From hee's father," he replied as he pointed to his kneeling employee.

"From his father?" I asked.

"Yes," he answered, "I leesen. He deedn't!"

"Feel" from the Horse's Standpoint

Because it is a prey animal that primarily relies upon flight to survive, the horse is one of the most sensually perceptive of all creatures. Its senses are able to detect stimuli such as smells, sounds, and sights that we, as predatory creatures, are incapable of detecting. Moreover, the horse *reacts* to these stimuli, to which we may be entirely oblivious. Keep in mind that the horse's *preferred* reaction to frightening novel stimuli is flight.

The horse *detects* very subtle stimuli. This may be a slight change in our body position, or even in a part of our body such as our seat or our hands. Although the untrained horse may not *respond* to these detected subtle stimuli, it will, in time, if those stimuli become a *signal* for a desired response. Therefore, *we must start with small signals*, and then progressively increase their intensity until a response is obtained, and then *stop!* Reward by instantly releasing pressure!

Unfortunately, it is not human nature to start with a small signal. It is our nature to start with a *big* signal, which does not produce horses with *feel*—horses that are *light*—and extremely responsive to mere suggestion.

Let's give an example:

Suppose we want to teach a green colt to move forward from a standstill. The bold but inexperienced rider will kick vigorously or even spur the horse aggressively. The horse will indeed move forward, sometimes with more enthusiasm than we desire, but this is not the way to produce a horse with lightness and feel.

Instead, the good horseman will alter his seat position, think forward, create leg pressure, and *look* forward. The horse knows where you are looking. The horse feels all these actions but does not understand what we want. So, the horseman increases the pressure and adds pressure at the hindquarters with a slap, or the touch of a rope or a dressage whip. If the horse doesn't move forward, he increases the pressures until it *does* move

Arizona clinician Karen Scholl. The level of communication between her and her Andalusian is obvious. Note the soft loose rein. She rides with "feel."

forward, whereupon, the pressure is immediately released. Eventually, the early light stimuli will become a signal that stronger stimuli will come if the horse doesn't move forward. In minutes the horse is *conditioned* to move forward by the light signals.

This applies to everything—to stopping, to reining, to jumping, to driving.

STEVE JEFFERYS

In the Australian book *Great Working Horse Stories* by Angela Goode (ABC Books, 2002), there is a section describing trainer Steve Jefferys. During the 2000 Olympics in Sydney, he starred at the opening ceremonies with his trick stallion, Ammo, and another stallion, Jamieson, who performed during intervals at the dressage finals. To quote the author:

"Steve made hilarious mockery of the efforts of international riders by executing complex dressage movements such as pirouettes and collected trots with just a piece of string around Jamieson's neck. He further humiliates would-be experts by installing a dummy steering wheel on Jamieson's wither and 'driving' him like a push-button car through perfectly executed corners with correct flexion and perfect square halts."

Steve admonishes, "You have to leave the lesson when you have the upper hand. A lot of people don't recognize when that is accomplished."

Again, *start light*. If there is no response, increase the pressure progressively and patiently until a response occurs, and then reward generously by immediately stopping the pressure. The greatest mistake made by the novice trainer—and regrettably, too many experienced trainers—is when they get a desirable response to (in effect) say to the horse, "Good, now I want you to do it again and again!" After rewarding the horse by stopping the pressure, let the horse digest this information. Wait, *then* ask for the same response. Don't ask for too much in the beginning. If we are teaching the horse to back, be grateful for one step backward; be grateful even for *half* a step. Eventually, the horse will become conditioned to the signal. So, you can ask for a second step, and then a third. But always start with small signals. Increase the signal only if there is no response. The goal is to get, in time, a *maximum* response to a *minimum* signal.

Reward the slightest try by releasing the pressure. That's how lightness is developed. That's a horse with "feel."

CHAPTER NINE

Early Learning

I often regret coining the term "imprint training," not because it is inaccurate, but because it has become frequently misused. I often hear people say "I imprinted my horse to lead," or "I imprinted my colt as a yearling."

One *trains* a horse to lead. Training is *learning by reinforcement.* Imprinting is a predetermined form of learning. The newborn foal will attach to whatever it sees moving around it: Mom, other animals, you, or a wheelbarrow. It is a visual phenomenon, and it is present only for a short while after birth.

That's why I renamed my most recent video *Early Learning* rather than *Imprint Training* unlike my original video, *Imprint Training of the Foal*, and my original book, *Imprint Training of the Newborn Foal.**

I stumbled on this incredibly fast and indelible way of shaping equine behavior in 1959. I had a series of dystocia cases (obstetrical emergencies), requiring extensive handling and manipulation of the foals I delivered. Weeks later when I saw the foals again, I noted that they seemed unafraid of me, and accepted handling with much more docility than most minimally handled foals. Some of them seemed to recognize me and actually approached me.

---

* *Early Learning*, Video Velocity, 1995; *Imprint Training of the Foal*, Palomine Productions, 1986; *Imprint Training of the Newborn Foal*, Western Horseman, 1991

Being familiar with research done a generation earlier by Austrian scientist Konrad Lorenz who, working with newly hatched geese, recognized the imprinting phenomenon and coined the term "imprinting," I suspected that a similar phenomenon was occurring with these foals. After all, every species is related, and the basic principles of behavioral science seem to apply to most higher species.

I owned a Quarter Horse mare, and when she foaled I apprehensively tried an experiment. Instead of *minimizing* contact with the foal as I had always been advised by respected horsemen and in agricultural and veterinary colleges, I *maximized* contact. By the next day, it was obvious that I was on to something. I had never seen a foal as calm, responsive, or gentle.

I followed this initial session with occasional training sessions after the foal was a few days old, teaching it to lead, to tie, to accept an invasion of every body opening (a veterinarian realizes how important this is), to accept working on its feet, to accept pressure in the girth and saddle areas and, most important, to respond to my commands to move in various directions. I promptly labeled the procedure "imprint training" because it consisted of *training* during the *imprinting* period. At the time I was not aware that by doing so, I was also teaching the foal to *learn* during its critical learning times.

After imprint training two more of my foals, I started preaching the concept to my clientele. Although most rejected it, saying "We've never done it that way" or "We don't have time to do that," a *few* did adopt it, with invariable success. Eventually, I was asked to make a video and later write a book on the subject. The rest is history. After nearly half a century, it is in use all over the world. Eventually, it led to a second career for me after I retired from veterinary practice, lecturing and writing about equine behavior. However, there are still people who oppose foal training, even though leading clinicians such as Pat Parelli, Richard Shrake, Clinton Anderson, Steve Edwards, Monty Roberts, John Lyons, and others support it, do it successfully, and have even produced videos of their own that demonstrate their versions of foal training.

The opposition is not limited to horse trainers. There are even behavioral scientists who denigrate the method, although an increasing number within academia are accepting it.

Imprint training the newborn foal to flex head and neck laterally while the mare bonds with it.

The newborn foal now flexes its legs, head and neck lightly and easily. It has learned to yield.

Thirty-six hours of age. Foal is taught to lead using "fixed butt rope."

Forty-eight hours of age.
Foal leads willingly.

Foal is tested with electric clippers uneventfully at 5 days of age. The mare in the photo is not its dam. It is a different mare but she was also imprinted at birth.

Some of the opposition to foal training is due to bad experiences with improperly trained foals, some due to emotional reasons, misconception, myths and fallacious traditions, close-mindedness, and even because some "trainers" don't want to start gentle horses because it spoils their "bronc busting act."

I'd like to address these opposing arguments, not because I feel offended by disagreement, but because it discourages people from using the most efficient method of training horses that exists, and because it is unfair to the horse. There is no better way of starting this fearful, timid, flighty animal, and proving to it that we humans can be as important to it as its mother.

1. It's Immoral to Intervene Between Mare and Foal.

It is understandable that some women are agitated when a human handles the foal before the mare arises and claims it, even though human babies are, almost without exception, delivered and handled before the mother handles them. It seems to offend some deep maternal instinct and has been called "a sin against nature." However, the practice has absolutely *no* ill effects such as interfering with the bonding of mare and foal. It can actually prevent the too frequent occurrence of foal rejection by timid mares, especially those that have never seen a newborn foal before. The practice also will deter the rather common occurrence of mares becoming aggressive toward humans after foaling. It has been well established scientifically that mares that were themselves imprint trained at birth consistently accept the handling of their own foals years later with aplomb. In fact, they seem to approve of it and reassure their foals that this is "normal" and acceptable.

2. This Is Not Imprinting. It Is Socialization.

Frankly, I don't care what it is called. This criticism, invariably voiced by academic behaviorists, is in fact incorrect. Yes, socialization occurs in the days that follow foaling, as we work with the foal just as it socializes with

Imprinting a newborn common zebra foal. I finally got a chance to do this at Saddlerock Ranch, Malibu, California. Owner Tami Semler assists. The zebra mare is frantic and wild so we had to separate mare and foal for the procedure, after which mare and foal resumed normal relations.

other horses, but there is no question that actual imprinting occurs. I have seen the recognition and following response in countless foals I handled at birth, and I have also seen foals bonded to nonliving objects such as tractors and manure carts that they saw move right after foaling. Foals as old as four months of age will leave their dams and go to whatever has imprinted them.

3. Imprinted Foals Are Dull and Unresponsive.

I believe that some people have overdone desensitization procedures, repeating them endlessly, and not doing them as I recommend, and have indeed "numbed" their foals to stimuli. However, this is a rare occurrence. Training foals, like training mature horses, *must* be done correctly to obtain good results. If done incorrectly, it isn't the fault of the method, but of the person doing the training.

The first mule ever trained as a newborn foal was my mule, Jordass Jean, foaled in 1980. She is the only mule ever invited to do exhibition jumping at an Olympic event (Los Angeles, 1984). She usually won or at least placed in every class she entered. She never refused to jump in her life. The mule industry is the most enthusiastic convert to imprint training and many breeders believe that without it, the current enthusiasm for mules would not have occurred. Here my daughter, Laurel, is shown on Jeanie at the 1984 Olympics.

Horses in every known equine discipline and of every breed have been trained at birth and have gone on to become superb performance champions. In fact, the very foals in both of the videos I have made on this subject went on to become winners on the racetrack (Thoroughbred), the show ring (Arabian, Peruvian Paso, and Quarter Horse), and steeplechase in Ireland (Thoroughbred).

4. Imprint Trained Foals Are Disrespectful.

Yes, this can happen if the training is done incorrectly, especially when only the birth session is performed but the subsequent lessons during which respect is obtained are not done. Interestingly, this mistake is made exclusively, in my experience, by women, in contrast to the following.

5. Imprint Training Does Not Work and the Foals So Trained Are Flightier and More Difficult to Handle.

This mistake, made exclusively by men, in my experience, is the result of haste during the first postpartum session. When desensitizing the newborn foal, one cannot do too many stimuli to induce habituation (acceptance of the stimulus), but one can definitely do too few. You must take the necessary time to do it correctly.

6. We Have Never Done It That Way.

Right! So, why change? The answer is—because it's better!

7. We Don't Have the Time.

There is *nothing* that can be done to save more time later on (and to prevent injuries to both people and horse) than to properly imprint train the newborn foal.

Racehorse breeders, in both flat racing and harness racing, have told me that the training time necessary when the horse is ready to go to the track has been reduced by 75 percent when the foals have been imprint trained.

8. I Just Don't Like It.

This comment comes most often from a few clinicians who have never personally tried foal imprinting, who have been presented with spoiled horses supposedly imprint trained, or who cherish their round pen bronc busting act of taking a frightened, flighty green colt and impressing their audiences by converting the "bronc" into a placid, cooperative horse in remarkably short time.

Admittedly, it is very impressive to watch this ritual, and it is dramatic evidence of the efficacy of natural horsemanship. But, understand that the newborn foal has the flight instincts and the fear that an unbroken two-year-old has. What we do with either determines that horse's attitude and responses henceforth. Imprinting is *equally* challenging, but it is so much faster and so much easier to imprint the newborn. There are two additional advantages:

1. You don't need to override previous learning, previous fears, and previous bad experiences.

2. The powerful imprinting phenomenon—the bond and desire to follow—can only be obtained in the newborn.

Clinicians like Pat Parelli, Monty Roberts, Richard Shrake, Richard Winters, Steve Edwards, Chris Cox, and others who support foal training are just as much cowboys as the clinicians who oppose it. After all, if it's

Monty Roberts and I discuss one of the orphaned mule deer fawns he found and imprinted.

a "Wild West Show" we want, why not do as we used to do: choke 'em down, forcibly restrain them, saddle them up, and buck them out?

Haven't we gone beyond that?

○ ○ ○

I have repeatedly asserted that I did not originate foal training. A narrative poem in Argentina describes the training of a newborn foal by a Native American. Stories and paintings cite that Bedouins took newborn foals into their tents and handled them.

Some years ago an older horseman named Harold Wadley contacted me.* He had seen my foal training video and wanted me to know that, when he grew up on the Cherokee Reservation in Oklahoma, his grandfather taught him a method called spirit blending, wherein the pregnant mare is handled daily starting a week or so prior to foaling, the handler speaking to her belly so the foal will know his voice. After foaling the foal is handled much as I do in my imprint training procedure.

---

* Wadley eventually published a book, *Spirit Blending Foals Before and After Birth* (Trafford Publishing, Victoria, Canada, 2003).

Debby and me with an imprinted rhinoceros in Kenya. To protect the rhinos from poachers, a guard armed with a rifle and a radio is with each animal 24 hours a day on the Ol Pojeta half million acre ranch. When a rhino calf is born, the guard handles it before the mother arises and claims it.

In 2004 I met a young man named Richard Earley at a horse expo. He watched my foal training video, and then told me that his grandfather and great-grandfather on the Cherokee Reservation had taught him a similar method. I asked him what they called it and he answered, "spirit blending." He did not know Wadley and was unfamiliar with his book. So, although I coined the name "imprint training" and have done all I can to popularize the method and explain its scientific rationale, I have no illusions that I invented anything. Many people in many parts of the world have done this before me.

Trainers the world over have taken this concept and elaborated upon it, adding to it in ways that I had not thought of before. Ole Johansen, a Norwegian harness horse trainer, teaches baby foals to drive, greatly facilitating their training period before racing. Allen Pogue, a trick horse trainer in Austin, Texas, has his baby foals doing incredible things. Marge Spencer of Norco, California, developed a harness with which she teaches baby foals to lead, to back, and to drive. She calls it the C M Lead and Drive Training System. Clinicians Monty Roberts, Clinton Anderson, and Pat Parelli have all added innovations to my basic system. All of the aforementioned people have made commercially available videos demonstrating their techniques.

Countless other breeders and trainers have adopted foal training as a routine part of their protocol. Illustrious Thoroughbred trainer D. Wayne Lukas told me at Churchill Downs, during derby week in 2004, "It's the only way. It's common sense."

He is correct.

CHAPTER TEN

Even Clinicians Make Mistakes

I do not intend to evaluate the clinicians in this chapter in order to denigrate them or criticize them negatively. These people have done an immeasurable service to the horse and to all of us who work with horses. All of the clinicians who have created this revolution in horsemanship are remarkable people. They are intelligent, because it took intelligence to adopt methods that are often contrary to human instinct and human nature and to convert to methods that are more natural and more acceptable to the horse.

They are courageous, because especially in the early decades of the revolution, but even now, the clinicians are subjected to derision, criticism, and scorn by many traditional horsemen. They are open-minded, or they would never have tried these different and often radical methods. They are kind and considerate, or these gentler and more humane methods would never have appealed to them. They have a desire—often a compulsion—to share what they have learned. This generosity is why they are good teachers. How unlike the traditional trainers of the past, most of whom (but not all) were secretive and jealously guarded their methods.

However, we all make mistakes. None of us is infallible, and, being human, the clinicians do criticize each other. They also often make inaccurate comments. Let's repeat some of those comments here, and examine their validity:

1. "I am not a predator."

Yes, you are! A predatory species is a hunting species, and we humans are hunters. Even in modern society, we display our predatory instincts in many ways. Sociologists say that gambling, a universal human pastime, is an outlet for the hunting instinct. We love target sports such as archery, billiards, bowling, and riflery. We love contact sports such as wrestling, boxing, and American football. We love goal sports such as hockey, soccer, basketball, and golf. Our most popular sports combine aspects of all of the aforementioned.

Humans most certainly *are* predators, but what I hope I have pointed out is that horses fear not so much the predator as predatory behavior. The clinicians have learned to suppress their predatory instincts and communicate with horses in a largely non-predatory way. This is no small achievement when one considers that the majority of the cowboy clinicians who launched the revolution in horsemanship were rodeo competitors. Moreover, as pointed out in my previous book, *The Revolution in Horsemanship,* many of them were rodeo champions.

2. "I don't want to dominate the horse. I want a partnership with him."

This is, of course, nonsense. We are in big trouble if the horse dominates the partnership.

Part of the misunderstanding comes from a misinterpretation of the word "dominate." In today's context many people take it to imply whips and chains. Yes, there *are* cruel dominant individuals. Al Capone was a dominant person. So were Adolf Hitler, Joseph Stalin, and Saddam Hussein.

But the most powerful dominant leaders in world history were *benevolent*, and their influence is more lasting than that of the cruel leaders. Jesus was dominant. So were Confucius, Buddha, Abraham Lincoln, George Washington, Thomas Jefferson, and Martin Luther King, Jr.

We *must* dominate the horse, but we can do it with empathy, gentleness, and kindness.

That's what this revolution is all about.

3. "I'm not here to entertain you."

We have heard this comment made to disparage clinicians, such as Pat

Parelli, who are highly entertaining. Pat once told us that he could teach any subject, even math, because a) he is a "ham" and keeps the students' attention, and b) he is enthusiastic.

Bull's-eye! Good teachers not only love their subject and love to share their knowledge, but they also have some kind of "act" to keep their students' attention. Parelli may use humor. Another uses the lariat in a fascinating Will Rogers sort of way. Others capitalize on their ethnic or social backgrounds. Their talents and their styles vary. Some students are drawn to one and despise another. It doesn't matter. They are all advancing the art and science of horsemanship.

4. "I don't care about you. I care about the horse!"

I don't believe this! I see an evangelical zeal, a desire to share information that indicates a concern for people as well as for the horse. All of the clinicians are intelligent enough and competent enough to have made a living in some other way. They chose to join the revolution because they have wanted a better deal for the horse, and also because they wanted to help others who are involved with horses. True disdain for people would show through, and the clinician who felt that way about his or her students would not succeed.

To be successful and effective practitioners, veterinarians must have great feelings for both people and animals. I often encounter young people who say that they aspire to become doctors of veterinary medicine because they love animals but hate people. If true, this attitude will guarantee failure, because the profession of veterinary medicine is as intimately involved with people as it is with animals. Similarly, to be an effective teacher of both horses and people, a clinician must have an affinity for both! To insist that one cares about the horse and has no regard for the human is a façade. One *cannot* be an effective teacher unless one has a rapport with one's student.

5. "He works too fast."

This criticism has been directed most frequently at Monty Roberts. Monty will step into a pen with a horse that is perhaps halter-broke, but still green and unridden. He stimulates flight, in both directions. In less than ten minutes, the horse has run its flight distance and is signaling submission and a desire to be led. Monty then becomes abruptly passive and non-threatening, and in less than half an hour he has the horse bonded to him, trusting him, and accepting a saddle, bridle, and rider with little or no fuss. It is done *quickly* because it is done *correctly*, utilizing body language understandable to the horse.

Speed is not the objective when working with horses, but if things are done correctly, it goes faster. The end result is what counts, and Monty's method is as effective as anyone else's in gaining the initial respect and bonding with the horse.

6. "There's nothing natural about natural horsemanship."

Some people have criticized the term "natural horsemanship," pointing out that nothing we do with horses is natural. Domestication is unnatural.

True, yet we believe the term is appropriate because this kind of horsemanship utilizes communication methods *natural* to the horse. These methods are:

A) Assertive threats that stimulate movement on the part of the horse. Control of movement establishes dominance in this species.

B) Stroking, which in a mutual-grooming species reassures and bonds. Note that we say "stroking," not "patting."

C) Advance and retreat, which in a flight species reassures, aborts the flight response, and desensitizes the horse to frightening stimuli.

D) Generous rewards. These reinforce desirable behavior with rest, stroking, reassurance, and praise, quickly conditioning the desirable responses.

E) Small signals that progressively increase the pressure until a response is obtained. The horse learns that if he does not respond to a small signal, a bigger one will follow. This progressive approach produces lightness.

F) Flooding, wherein horses swiftly habituate to frightening but harmless stimuli if they are rapidly and extensively repeated.

Regard the above list and one can see where "traditional horsemanship" is often lacking:

A) Excessive aggressiveness and infliction of pain, which *justifies* the horse's fear of humans.

B) Slapping or vigorously patting as a reward rather than gentle stroking.

C) Advancing, without retreating, which provokes flight—or fight.

D) Failure to flood, stopping the frightening stimulus prematurely, reinforces and fixes the flight reaction, and explains why so many horses are spooky, ear shy, head shy, afraid of electric clippers, and so on.

E) Starting with severe signals and later diminishing them, rather than vice versa. This all too common mistake comes to us naturally. We spur, or squeeze, or rein, or whip too hard initially, planning to later diminish our signals. This is backwards from the way it should be done, and it creates fear and distrust in the horse.

F) Demanding repetition of desirable behavior—such as a good stop, a good turn, or a good jump—without reinforcing rewards. This is the most common training mistake: immediately demanding a repeat performance or an even *better* one without some sort of reinforcement. Gifted horsemen emphasize the importance of *not* spoiling a lesson with endless repetitions.

Legendary trainer Jack Brainard says in his book, *If I Were to Train a Horse*,* "Boredom is primarily caused from too much repetition. Too

---

* Jack Brainard, *If I Were to Train a Horse*, Print Comm, Inc., Dallas, Texas, 2000.

many trainers don't know when to quit . . . It's a good idea to only work a few minutes on any particular movement." He then quotes the French trainer Francois Baucher, "Any cue or aid correctly applied will deaden a horse if used to excess."

The great contemporary trainer Eitan Beth-Halachmy, of Grass Valley, California, the founder of cowboy dressage, says, "If you and your horse get a given exercise right once or twice, quit right there and reward your horse. Do not drill or overtrain."

The words of these masters of horsemanship precisely verify the scientific principles of learning behavior.

Jack Brainard says in his book If I Were to Train A Horse *(Print Comm, Inc., Dallas, TX, 2000), "Boredom is primarily caused from too much repetition. Too many trainers don't know when to quit . . ."*

CHAPTER ELEVEN

Things We Don't Fully Understand

There are a number of techniques, none of which are new or completely original, but which are enjoying a wave of popularity associated with the revolution in horsemanship. These techniques are non-coercive in nature, which explains their acceptance by many horsemen, because rejecting coercive training techniques is currently in vogue. Let's examine some of these techniques, admitting that we don't understand why they work, although theories abound and are strongly expressed by their advocates. All these techniques have one thing in common: they involve the use of repetitious, rhythmic sensory stimuli. Whether the results obtained are due to the elaboration of endorphins by the brain, a mesmerizing or hypnotic effect, a submissive state produced by anxiety, a cataleptic state, or simply desensitization accompanied by socialization, the reasons remain unproven for now.

What *is* important is that they all work. The horse subjected to such methods *does* become calmer, more relaxed, less flighty, and therefore more responsive to us.

1. Poll Pressure

When the poll is pressed (where the skull joins the atlas at the first cervical vertebra), a horse can be quickly trained to lower its head. Is the resultant calmness caused by discouraging the flight position, with head raised? Or, does it work by mimicking the head-lowered submissive posture of this species? Or, does it promote the flow of endorphins? Maybe it just feels good, as a neck massage does to us.

2. Pressure Under the Upper Lip

I learned long ago that a lead chain placed under the upper lip of a horse will produce calmness and cooperativeness. Does this happen because it feels good, because of endorphin release, or simply because the horse knows that excruciating, paralyzing pain will be caused if severe pressure is put upon the chain? If the chain is vibrated, an even more profound effect is observed. Why?

It is significant that a tranquil state can almost invariably be quickly obtained by massaging under a horse's lip with the finger. Acupuncturists say that this area is an important pressure point.

I am rubbing the upper gums of a horse in order to elicit sedation before applying a twitch.

ACUPUNCTURE

Tom Watson, DVM, of Scottsdale, Arizona, is a trained acupuncturist whose patients include horses. He has noted that following the placement of several needles around the coronet of some horses, he has observed profound sedation. Acupuncturists have a variety of explanations for this phenomenon, but none of these explanations have been scientifically proven. Here's another phenomenon we do not yet fully understand.

3. The TTouch

Clinician and horsewoman Linda Tellington-Jones includes repetitious, circling massages of various parts of the horse's body as a part of her program. Performed as directed, this touching results in a state of relaxed calmness even by ordinarily fractious horses. Why? What is happening physiologically and neurologically? How does it relate to the previously described responses obtained with pressure under the lip, or to those that

Linda Tellington-Jones doing her TTouch on a horse's ear.

follow? Keep in mind that we are offering just a few examples here. There are many others. For example, manipulation of the ear can produce a variety of reactions. A traditional example is "earing down" a bronc, an old cowboy trick. Severe pressure on an ear, including biting the tip of it, will temporarily subdue a majority of wildly excited horses. Why? A physiologist might say the response is due to "inhibition through pain," working as a twitch does on the upper lip of a horse. (See the photo on page 83.)

An acupuncturist, however, might explain the result differently, citing meridians and acupressure points. We really don't know the reason. Gentle massage of the ear, conversely, will often sedate a horse. It works, but why?

4. The Endo-Stick

J. P. Giacomini, an international horseman now residing in Lexington, Kentucky, developed the Endo-Stick, a semi-rigid fiberglass stick with a rubber or gel-filled ball at one end. The horse is rhythmically tapped with the ball. The horse is soon habituated to this stimulus and then goes into a state of relaxation.

Trick horse trainer Allen Pogue, of Austin, Texas, uses a version of the Endo-Stick extensively in his novel and effective routines.

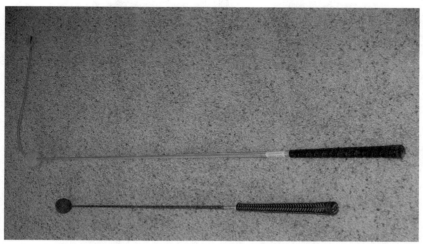

J.P. Giacomini's Endo-Stick and a personal variation of it by Allen Pogue, a trick horse trainer from Austin, Texas,.

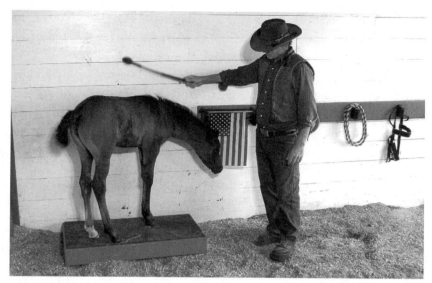

Allen Pogue, tapping a foal's withers with Giacomini's Endo-Stick, elicits a submissive, calm, lowered head position.

○ ○ ○

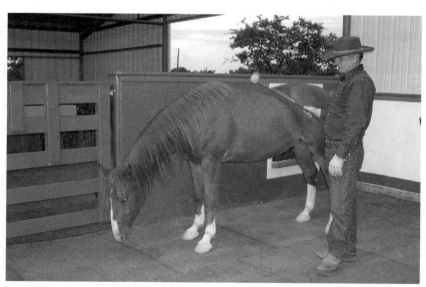

Allen Pogue taps the withers of a mature horse with Giacomini's Endo-Stick eliciting a submissive attitude and lowered head position.

Observe that all of the cited methods involve repetitious tactile stimuli. The response is by no means restricted to horses. It can be demonstrated in other species, including our own.

Dr. Robert K. Anderson, a veterinarian who is noted for his work in canine behavior and is a professor emeritus at the University of Minnesota College of Veterinary Medicine, was instrumental in the development of the head collar for training dogs. He states that poll pressure is one of the reasons this device so quickly modifies the behavior of a disrespectful or fractious dog.

As I said, there is a lot we do not yet fully understand, but theories and opinions abound.

May I offer a hypothesis?

About one year before I began writing this book, I was in my automobile in a line of traffic, waiting for the red stoplight to turn green. I suddenly became aware of a deep throbbing that I felt more than I heard. Most of us have experienced that sensation, caused by the bass on a car stereo turned up to maximum volume. I could not hear the music, only the throbbing percussion. Looking about for the driver (who I suspected would be wearing a baseball cap backwards), I soon located him behind

Dr. R. K. Anderson's headcollar for dogs, the Gentle Leader, is based on experience with horses.

me and to my right. Then I realized that the sound I was hearing and feeling was familiar.

Lub dub, lub dub, lub dub.

I had heard that sound countless thousands of times through my stethoscope as I examined kittens, calves, mature horses, elephants, dolphins, and even birds. It was the sound of a beating heart.

This realization set me thinking. No one is more aware of the power of learning in the newborn than I am. Utilizing this phenomenon led me to "imprint training," in use all over the world not only in foals, but in the newborns of many other precocial species.

Is it possible that the heartbeat of the mother, loudly transmitted through the placental fluids, is imprinted prenatally upon the unborn young? Isn't that why a puppy, removed from its mother and its littermates, is comforted by a ticking alarm clock? The effects of imprinting last a lifetime. Is that why we humans have such an affinity for music? Primitive peoples' first musical instrument is a drum of some kind. Is that a desired sound because it returns us to the comfort of the womb?

Most popular music has a percussive beat. Even uneducated people love popular music.

Classical music, as a general rule, does not have a percussive beat. No heart sounds. Is that why the musically uneducated masses are not, as often, attracted to the classics?

If music, especially percussion, is a throwback to the uterine environment, why are we the only mammal to make music? Perhaps because we are the only really complex tool users, and tools are needed to make music. However, I have seen primitive tribesmen chant and clap their hands in the absence of any musical instruments, but then our hands are *designed* to use tools.

The fetus in the uterus does not only hear the heartbeat of its mother, it *feels* it. The rhythm is constant, never stopping. Secure in the womb, the fetus hears and feels only the heartbeat. The vibrations of the beating heart must readily transmit through the placental fluids. The frequency only varies with the size of the mother and her state of activity. The late term fetus *must* be imprinted with both the sound and feel of the heartbeat.

Can this be the reason that rhythmic tapping with Giacomini's Endo-Stick consistently evokes relaxation? And is it all relaxation or is it submission? The horse's head always drops, which signals submission. Do the rhythmic circles of Tellington-Jones' TTouch emulate the liquid waves of placental fluid produced by the maternal heartbeat?

To calm their stallions, horsemen through the centuries have rhythmically vibrated lead ropes, reins, and their own legs when mounted. They hiss, or whistle repetitiously and rhythmically. They rub their horses. Why is massage so soothing? Why do repetitious, rhythmic sounds mesmerize us?

Is it possible that it can all be explained by what the Austrian scientist, Konrad Lorenz, observing how newly hatched goslings bonded to what they saw moving around them, called "*prägungs*" (imprint). From "*Prägen*" (to stamp or impress).

If so, the rocking cradle suddenly makes sense. Why do we rhythmically bounce the fretting baby? Why do we change our voice when speaking to a small child or a pet? Are we instinctively muffling our voice to make it sound more like it would to an unborn fetus? Why do we do these things? Could it be because they work?

We are told that horses react to steady pressure by pressing back, which every colt starter learns. But horses respond to intermittent pressure by *yielding*. Constant pressure evokes counter-pressure. It evokes obstinacy. Intermittent pressure—a rhythmic, repeated *tactile* stimulus—evokes *response*. These questions and hypothesis offer an explanation for many horse reactions: why unyielding and extreme contact produces a "hard mouth," and why soft fingers and supple reins produce a "soft mouth." Why horses that pull back when tied firmly panic and pull back even more violently, while horses tied to something that gives, like elastic, do not. Why horses resent a girth fully tightened all at once, but will tolerate one drawn up to the same pressure in increments.

Experienced horsemen know these things. What we have to learn is *why*, because there is always an explanation for why horses respond as they do, even if we are now ignorant of that explanation.

CHAPTER TWELVE

They Don't Whisper

When Nicholas Evans published his best-selling novel, *The Horse Whisperer,* in 1996, which inspired the motion picture of the same name, he revived a term that had been lost in antiquity.

In late eighteenth-century Ireland, a man named Dan Sullivan became famous for taming vicious or uncontrollable horses with a method that mystified society at that time. Sullivan would isolate himself with the problem horse in an enclosed barn or stall. Curious onlookers could not see what he was doing, and they heard only his voice softly speaking to the horse. What they couldn't see was what he *must* have been doing; he was controlling the horse's movements with one or more of the methods described earlier. Hence, they assumed that the power lay in his voice and they dubbed him "The Whisperer."

In time, the term spread throughout the British Isles. *The Oxford Universal Dictionary's* 1933 edition defines "whisperer" as "an appellation for certain horse-breakers, said to have obtained obedience by whispering to the horse."

Evans' book and the subsequent movie popularized the term in America. The clinicians involved in the launching of the revolution in horsemanship had nothing to do with the term "horse whisperer." Neither did Buck Brannaman, the clinician hired as a technical advisor for the movie, nor his assistant, clinician Curt Pate, refer to himself by that name. They don't whisper.

In fact, with rare exceptions, nearly all of the clinicians teaching natural horsemanship decry the term because it is inaccurate. "Whispering" smacks of mysticism, but none of the good clinicians suggest that they have any mystical powers. They all understand that they are effective because they have learned how to best communicate with the horse. They all tell their students that, if they have the motivation, they too can learn this kind of horsemanship; ordinary people can obtain extraordinary results. All it requires is knowledge and desire.

However, we *can* communicate with horses vocally, and this concept needs to be explored. We humans and the animals we are most closely involved with communicate mainly in two ways: we vocalize and we use body language. Dogs, for example, bark, yelp, whine, and growl—all vocalizations directed at another individual's sense of hearing. Dogs also use body language directed at another individual's sense of vision. They stand tall, snarl, fix their gazes, and erect their body hairs to menace. They wag their tails and lower their forequarters as an invitation to play. They lie down, fold their forepaws, and sometimes smile to signal submission.

We humans also use body language. The form it takes and our understanding of it is genetically established. In all human cultures, the open hand is a sign of peace; the upraised fist is a threat; the bowed head signals submission. That's why we bow in respect and bow in prayer. We nod "yes" in acquiescence. We fold our arms and stand erect in defiance. We crouch in fear.

Surely, *no* species is more dependant upon vocalization for communicating than we are. The ranting at a sports event or a political rally, the din at a cocktail party, the shouts of a drill sergeant or of a yard full of children at play are familiar examples. Today, in fact, vocal communication is becoming more common when people are alone than when they are with others. I am referring, of course, to the ubiquitous cell phone.

Verbal language, frequently but not necessarily accompanied by body language, is overwhelmingly the primary method by which we communicate. Inevitably, when working with animals, we are inclined to use *our* language in an attempt to communicate: "Bad boy! Good boy! No! Yes! Good girl! Bad girl! No! Yes! No!"

Horses have excellent hearing, capable of detecting a range of sounds beyond the capacity of the human ear and then localizing those sounds with the aid of their mobile directional ears. Moreover, horses do communicate with each other with a variety of sounds including whinnying, squealing, and nickering. But, horses depend primarily upon body language for communication. Because they are prey animals, excessive noise may attract predators. Thus, another incompatibility between horse and human: one prefers body language, and the other prefers speech.

Auditory signals *can* be used very effectively as an adjunct to communication with horses. Clicker training is widely used as a bridging stimulus, linking a command and a behavior in sea mammals, primates, dogs, and many other species. Clicker training works well with horses. In *The Revolution in Horsemanship* we described the work of killer-whale trainer Shawna Karrasch, who achieves marvelous results with her On Target Training. It combines training a horse to respond to a clicker and then interpreting the sound as a reward, with touching a mobile target and using food treats for positive reinforcements.

Horsemen throughout history have used verbal sounds to let the horse know what is expected, or to let the horse know that it did the right—or wrong—thing. So, we cluck, we click, we whistle, we chirp, we say "whoa," we say "trot" or "walk," and so on. The first horses I worked with as a boy were draft horses trained to work entirely with verbal commands like "Gee" (turn right), "Haw" (turn left), "Whoa," "Get up" (go forward), or "Back."

But we humans are a verbose lot, and therein lies the problem. We say too much and thereby lose the value of verbal commands. "Whoa" should mean only one thing: "Stop!" It should be said only once and it should never mean "slow down." To slow down, the command "easy" can be used or even "slow down." Repetitiously saying "Whoa, whoa, whoa, whoa" simply desensitizes the horse to the term to the point where it means nothing. Watch clinicians like Richard Winters, Monty Roberts, Clinton Anderson, or Dennis Reis. They stop their horses with a change in their seat position, perhaps a subtle rein signal, and a sharply uttered but soft "Whoa!"

Many horsemen cluck or click their tongues or make a hissing sound as a signal for a specific behavior. That's fine! It works just like the clicker.

But, constantly and endlessly clicking or clucking completely desensitizes the horse to that sound so that its only function is to entertain the one doing the clucking, or to serve as a form of displacement behavior—a safety valve if you will—for the person doing the training. (Maybe that's where the term "dumb cluck" came into use!)

Clinician Pat Parelli, in his school of horsemanship (Parelli Natural Horse-Man-Ship) does not allow his students to use verbal commands until they reach the third level of his program. I once challenged this policy, pointing out that verbal commands can serve as a useful tool in the stimulus-response relationship, and as positive reinforcement for desired behavior, providing that it is used correctly.

His answer was memorable: "We humans primarily communicate verbally. In order to teach students to communicate with horses using body language, I discourage verbal language by students in their early horsemanship. This forces them to exaggerate their body language and helps them to communicate. Later on, they can add verbal commands once they have become adept at using body language."

Even though we humans have by far the most complex and extensive vocal communication, some species communicate via sound far more than do horses. For example, the rumbling of elephants has been found to be an elaborate communication system, as have varied sounds emitted by sea mammals like dolphins and whales. Horses, then, are a relatively quiet species, but, not as quiet as other prey animals like the giraffe, for example. Fortunately, we humans can reason, and we can be taught the optimum way to communicate with horses, but it doesn't necessitate whispering. Occasionally, when I meet people, they ask, "Are you the Doctor Miller who is the horse whisperer?"

I like to respond by screaming as loud as I can, "YES!"

CHAPTER THIRTEEN

The Myth of Native Horsemanship

I have seen firsthand the horsemanship of societies that laud and idolize their native horsemen and their traditional training methods. These include the *gauchos* of Argentina, the horsemen of Peru, the *charros* of Mexico, the *guardiens* of the French Camargue, the Bedouins of the Middle East, the jackaroos and bushmen of Australia, the *paniolos* of Hawaii, American Indian tribesmen, the horsemen of various Caribbean Islands, and, of course, the cowboys of Canada and the United States.

I have had the opportunity to ride with many of the above-named horsemen and observed their methods at various times in my life. Infatuated by the legends I had heard and read about their prowess, I was disillusioned to actually see some of their methods in use.

They are all wonderful riders but *crude* horsemen, except for occasionally gifted individuals. All, to a greater or lesser extent, use unnecessary and excessive force. There is unwarranted dependence upon such tools as bits, spurs, and whips, all *legitimate* tools, but excessively and improperly used in native horsemanship worldwide. Even in traditional Californio vaquero horsemanship, many routine practices were unnecessarily harsh. Today's natural horsemanship clinicians are getting *better* results with gentler, more humane, and scientifically sound methods.

In Argentina, the most horse-oriented country I have ever been in, and where there is immense pride in their gaucho horsemanship, unbroken colts are haltered and tied to a log for a day or longer to teach them to respect the halter. Does it work? Yes! But are some colts irreparably injured doing this? Yes! Is it necessary? No! Absolutely not!

It is common to apply a short twitch to the lip of a colt, tie it to the bridle, and then ride the horse on the assumption that this crude idea will make the horse gentler. I saw a Thoroughbred colt at the Buenos Aires training track twitched in this manner, saddled, warmed up, breezed on the track, cooled out, and the twitch removed one hour and ten minutes after it had been applied.

Colts that shied were whipped mercilessly for a prolonged period of time, learning nothing. I rode a wonderful Criollo horse that freaked out when I slapped at a mosquito on my neck. It took ten minutes for him to calm down, and then he exploded again when I slapped at another mosquito on my wrist, all the result of excessive use of the quirt.

In Hawaii years ago, a colt breaker on a huge cattle ranch told me that the first thing he does when starting a colt is to slam it over the head with a fence post to try to knock it to the ground. Thank goodness, many of the mainland clinicians have been to Hawaii and have caused a change in such brutal methods. These were widespread in Hawaii not too long

Since its inception, Western Horseman *magazine has chronicled the advancement of western horsemanship. An article by Joe de Yong dramatically describes the frontier-born methods of colt breaking when it was published in 1949. Any reader of this same magazine today over half a century later, will note the very different methods now being used to start colts. This article, and the author's vivid illustrations, attest to the success of "the revolution in horsemanship."*

ago, the result of misunderstanding. In 1832 three vaqueros were brought to Hawaii to teach the natives how to rope and ride in order to harvest the thousands of wild cattle and horses that had been introduced into the islands and multiplied into vast herds. The paniolos (a corruption of the word "Español") learned well. They are superb cowboys, roping and riding hard in the roughest of country. Their methods, however, until recently, have been brutally harsh. Once today's clinicians started visiting Hawaii and demonstrating natural horsemanship, things began to change rapidly. In addition to the visiting mainland clinicians, Hawaii has at least two resident clinicians who have had a beneficial influence. These are Lester Buckley on the Big Island and David Carswell on Kauai.

○ ○ ○

A horse breaker on a Southern Arizona ranch in 1948, when I was twenty-one years of age, led me to a search for better methods of horsemanship. I said to him, "Gee, I'd surely like to know how to break colts."

"Sure!" he responded, "I'll show you!"

He selected a very gentle three-year-old gelding; showed me how to halter-break it; how to "double" it three times in each direction, letting it run away and then jerking it around "so the nose will be sore tomorrow from the hackamore and he'll want to turn," he added. This colt was so lazy and indifferent that he never bucked when I mounted him. I rode him for three days, working on a fence line.

My mentor finally asked, "Hey, how is the colt doing?"

I whined, "I can turn him to the left, but he won't turn right. If I want to go right, I have to make a 360 degree turn to the left."

"Show me," he suggested.

I demonstrated my incompetence and the colt's inability to turn right, his feet glued to the ground. Of course, I had no idea how to use the hackamore. I just pulled and pulled without results.

"I'll fix him," my teacher said.

He tied the colt down on the ground and rasped his forefeet down to the bloody quick with a shoeing rasp. I was familiar with this trick. It was supposed to encourage the colt to turn on his hindquarters. I didn't realize then what a pathetic substitute it was for skill.

Then, he picked up a melon-sized rock and pounded the right side of the colt's neck. I winced in sympathy as I saw the pain and alarm in the colt's eyes because, although he had frustrated me, I liked his gentle nature and had bonded with him.

The colt breaker then rolled the horse over and began to pound the left side of his neck. "He's okay there," I protested. "He turns to the left."

I was ignored so I put my hand on the man's shoulder and said, "No, he's okay on that side."

The colt breaker stood up and angrily said, "You don't want to learn? To hell with you!" He threw the rock to the ground.

The colt did turn to the right the next day. I had worked on the historic Irvine Ranch the preceding summer, where I had seen my first California reined stock horses. I didn't know how such horses were created, but I did know that it wasn't done by rasping feet down until they were painfully tender, nor by bruising neck muscles to eliminate all resistance. Thus I began my lifelong search for more refined, gentler, and more intelligent methods of communicating with horses so they will do what we want them to do, and do it willingly.

Many years later, I was in the Middle East and thrilled to the sight of two Bedouins racing my car alongside a desert road. I then saw the gaping mouths and elevated noses of their Arabian horses and the severe rein contact. My admiration was quickly dashed.

Wherever I have gone to experience, with anticipation, native horsemanship, I have been disappointed. Invariably, unnecessary coercive methods and frank cruelty have shattered my romanticized illusions.

I must admit that, in every place where I saw crude horsemanship, I also saw methods that *were* admirable, and I learned *good* things from each of those horse cultures. In Argentina, for example, where so much of the gaucho horsemanship is excessively brutal, they also have some great tricks. I saw a horse wrangler on a large cattle station ride up to a herd of horses of all sizes and ages and shout, "*Forme!*" The horses, out in a large pasture, all lined up facing in the same direction, waiting for the gauchos to select and halter the one they wanted. This is an apparently common method in Argentina, better than herding the horses into a corral and roping the ones wanted, a common method on the larger American ranches. I have heard of a South Texas ranch that uses this Argentine system.

We all have a lot to learn from each other.

None of these people were intentionally cruel, I am sure. They simply were doing what they had been taught and what had become traditional. I'm also sure that many of them had a great love and admiration for horses.

Horsemen in general cling to tradition. After all, we have made a primarily archaic beast an important part of our lives. We are backward-looking people. As a veterinarian, I have been in the homes of countless horse owners. Rarely will one see modern or contemporary furnishings or decor. Horse people lean toward traditional styling: Colonial, Western, Southwestern, Alpine. We horse people *are* backward-looking, and we cling to the obsolete animal we love and an ancient technology.

This affection for tradition is admirable in many ways, but it often causes us to be closed-minded and reluctant to accept new ideas. I see that in myself, and have disciplined myself to maintain an attitude of what I call "open-minded skepticism." I urge all horsemen to maintain that attitude. Do not blindly accept new concepts, but *be willing to try them*. Evaluate them fairly. Except for such an attitude, civilization could not progress. Never stop learning. I have handled countless thousands of horses in my life, of every possible description, but I am still learning. I don't think I have ever conducted a clinic or a seminar at which I failed to learn something I didn't know before. Sometimes the horse was my teacher, and sometimes it was someone in the audience.

Many people, including me, assumed that classical European horsemanship was free of brutality, which is so prevalent in native horsemanship. Unfortunately, this is not true. In recent years, visiting Europe, I have learned that even in some world-class stables, using horses of superb breeding, extremely cruel and unnecessarily forceful methods are routinely used.

Ed Connell recorded for posterity the methods of the Californios — The California Vaquero. His books, *Reinsman of the West — Bridles and Bits* and *Hackamore Reinsman* are classics, available today from Lennoche Publishers of Wimberly, Texas. More recently

Lennoche has published *Vaquero Style Horsemanship*, a compilation of articles and letters by and about Ed Connell.

The horsemanship that evolved in colonial California, originating in Morocco, and migrating to Spain, and then to Mexico, led to the most sophisticated form of native horsemanship the world has ever known. Yet it included elements of harshness which today's natural horsemanship clinicians have eliminated completely. *Vaquero Style Horsemanship*, especially, describes forceful methods which were deemed necessary and traditional in the past, but which have been replaced by psychological methods which work more rapidly, more safely, and even more effectively.

The very best clinicians have combined the California vaquero method with classical European horsemanship to achieve the incredible results seen today.

CHAPTER FOURTEEN

Horses Are Copycats

Imitative behavior is common in the animal kingdom. As proof, try this: When your dog is in quiet repose in your home, sit up suddenly, assume a position of alarm, and sharply say, "What's that? What's that?" Most dogs will immediately mirror your attitude of concern and "woof" in alarm or warning. Dogs, a species that always lives in groups in the wild, readily mirror their pack leader's attitude and actions.

Horses, which always live in groups, also will mirror their companion's behavior. In fact, this phenomenon is even more profound in horses than in dogs because horses are a prey species. Responding to stimuli as a unit reduces the risk of being killed and eaten by a predatory carnivore.

When one horse in a group wheels and flees in alarm, the rest of the group responds similarly. When a veterinarian arrives at a stable, the word quickly goes around and all the inmates are notified. For this reason, when I had to treat a group of horses at a stable, I always worked with the gentler and calmer ones first. To start with an excitable, fractious individual would create an alarm reaction, which would make all of the others more difficult to work with. It is interesting to watch a foal cantering alongside its mother, very frequently matching her exact stride, in a perfect cadence. This synchronized reaction is an expression of what is known as *allelomimetic behavior*: imitative behavior, most dramatic in creatures that live in groups.

Perhaps the best example of copycat behavior may be seen in our own children. Their behavior is modeled by what they see their parents do, and also, unfortunately, by what they see in the entertainment media and the behavior of their peers.

The behavior of horses—or perhaps we should say the misbehavior—often reflects the behavior of the person handling or riding the horse. An aggressive handler may create difficulty by causing fear of that handler. What do novice riders do if the horse they are riding shies or bolts? They clutch up, assume a fetal position, grab with their legs, jerk on the reins, and often yell or scream. A tense or a fearful rider or even an apprehensive or nervously reactive rider can cause a horse to be fearful and flighty, not because the horse fears that person, but because fear is contagious. The horse doesn't fear the rider, but fears whatever it is that the rider fears. In the wild, this contagious fearfulness contributes to the horse's survival.

But shouldn't the opposite also be true, that a quiet, composed, relaxed and calm handler will be more likely to elicit similar behavior in his equine subjects? And don't we see this, in effect, at all the leading clinicians' clinics?

One of Pat Parelli's promotional videos, *Discover the Secrets of Success With Horses*, shows several dramatic examples of copycat behavior in

Clinician Linda Parelli demonstrates what is called "allelomimetic" (copycat) behavior. Young foals often display this when following their dams, as do teams of draft horses.

horses. The mimicked behavior in this video is desirable. When led from the ground, the horses mimic the gaits of the persons leading them, even changing leads with them. Horses emulate the movements of their human leaders, even when the movements are extremely subtle. Also, the relaxed, non-confrontational attitudes of the humans are reflected by their equine subjects. Importantly, when the human assumes a playful attitude, the horses respond with playfulness.

We like to play. Horses like to play as well and, in any species, work is most acceptable when it takes the form of play. Consider that many of the things we do for *pleasure* actually require hard physical effort. Riding is an example, but even more demanding are skiing, surfing, scuba diving, rock climbing, cycling, jogging, skating, or swimming. All of these require hard physical effort. They are even risky. Yet we pursue such sports with passion and even *pay* to do them.

Horses can be trained the same way. They are athletic creatures who, in nature, stay alive by running away from perceived danger. Therefore, they needn't be literally *forced* to jump, or race, or cut, or pen, or rope, or gather and drive cattle. It shouldn't be necessary to use coercion to get a horse to do pole bending, or pull a cart, or prance in parades, or do a piaffe or a pirouette. *If* these things are presented as play, and *if* the relationship between horse and human is that of herd leader and herd subordinate, and *if* the human creates a willingness in the horse to perform the desired task, the horse should *want* to do it. Isn't this the same reason why dogs retrieve and race through strenuous agility courses and joyously herd livestock? They *want* to do those things because skilled trainers can encourage this attitude.

What defines a good scout leader, an effective school teacher, or an inspiring athletic coach is the ability to make his or her charges *want* to perform, *want* to excel, *want* to win. Horses are no different. Who has accomplished more in human progress, the slave who worked to avoid being physically punished or the voluntary worker who works for personal reward? Slaves have been forced to do work throughout history, but most of the progress in civilization was achieved by people who were motivated not by fear, but by desire for rewards. Horses are the same. They *can* be slaves and usually have been throughout history. But, they can also be partners, members of our team. It's all in how they are taught. The method used and the choice are up to us.

CHAPTER FIFTEEN

Chimpanzees

What in the world is a chapter about chimpanzees doing in a book about horses?

Bear with me and you will see.

When I retired from my career of practicing veterinary medicine in 1987 at the age of sixty, I did not plan on a second career writing about, lecturing on, and teaching animal behavior. I had been doing these things sporadically since 1962 and I assumed that these activities would continue, but I did not foresee the explosion of interest in the revolution in horsemanship. This interest has taken me to every continent and given me the enormous gratification of seeing what many considered to be radical ideas become accepted procedures throughout the horse industry.

As I reflect upon my life from the vantage point of old age, I realize that I've had an interest in animal behavior since boyhood. I taught my dogs all sorts of tricks, like leaping through my arms, which I held to form a hoop. In my mid-twenties I was "breaking" colts (we who do not whisper prefer to call it colt "starting") using what we now call natural horsemanship.

Moreover, what were then known as "colts" were four- to six-year-old horses that had never been close to a human being. These were horses born in the wild. The only human contact for some of them was to be captured as yearlings, their forelegs roped with a lariat, tripped, thrown, tied down, branded, and if they were male, gelded without benefit of anesthesia.

Using patience and kindness, I taught these colts to accept handling, to accept a lead, to tolerate a hackamore and saddle. After an hour a day for a week or so, I was able to mount them in a confined round pen, and they never bucked. After three or four rides in the pen, I'd ride them in a large corral a few times. They then would go right out gathering and driving cattle, which was where they really got their education, because I was a completely untrained and unskilled horseman.

It seems ridiculous now, but I would never allow anyone to watch me start colts because I was embarrassed. It wasn't "macho," and my petting and talking to the colts were not the traditional cowboy way. I would explain that if anyone was present it would divert the colt's attention from me, so I had to work alone. At one ranch I worked, the owner and some other employees tried to watch me through binoculars to see how I could start such colts without having them buck.

I spent all of my student summers like that. At thirty years of age I graduated veterinary school and never started another colt for anyone else except myself. However, I gradually brought the same principles into my horse practice, and in less than a decade after I graduated, I was being invited to demonstrate my methods of handling horses at veterinary meetings and conferences. Eventually, non-veterinary groups invited me to do clinics until such groups exceeded those at veterinary conferences.

The first time I saw a Ray Hunt clinic, in San Luis Obispo in the late 1970s, I decided to support and promote what I knew was to become a revolution in horsemanship. A decade later I made the difficult decision to abandon the fascinating, profitable, and satisfying career that I loved, and devote myself full time to the revolution.

○ ○ ○

I graduated from the veterinary school at Colorado State University in 1956, married a senior undergraduate student, Debby, who became my life partner, and we practiced for one year in Arizona. Seeking a group practice, I moved to California. Unable to find a practice as I conceived it to be, I created one in the Conejo Valley, in Ventura County, a huge, sprawling area between Los Angeles and Santa Barbara Counties.

There were two towns in the Conejo Valley: Newbury Park with a population of 600 people, and Thousand Oaks with fewer than 1,300 residents. There was no practicing veterinarian in the valley, but an enormous animal population, with veterinary services coming in from other areas outside the valley.

Thousands of beef cattle roamed the valley floor, attended by cowboys on hundreds of horses. There were prosperous racehorse farms, dog kennels, a mink ranch, and luxury ranches owned by movie and television stars. Western movies were filmed at several "sets." The valley residents, of course, had all sorts of house pets, backyard horses, and 4-H projects of pigs, goats, sheep, and rabbits. Someone imported and raised all kinds of birds. Ten miles away, in the town of Moorpark, was a flourishing poultry industry, including the world's largest egg farm with three million laying hens—and no vet!

Most exciting of all, and second only to horse and cattle ranching, the valley's largest industry was wild animals. Ventura County's zoning allowed the presence of an astounding variety of zoo animal facilities. There was a camel breeding farm, an elephant training center, and Jungleland. Jungleland served the entertainment industry and it housed, for example, forty male African lions. All of this was within walking distance from my office. The chorus at night was unforgettable. Behind our hospital was the John Strong Family Circus, and other circus acts also headquartered in town.

There was a severe shortage of veterinarians in those post World War II years, and many of my colleagues in Los Angeles County limited their practices to dogs and cats, horses, or dairy cattle. Willing to handle any creature, I soon had a thriving and unusual practice, which even included the whales and dolphins at Santa Monica's Pacific Ocean Park.

Our community grew, and our practice grew so that, when I retired in 1987, our group consisted of twelve veterinarians. But the latter half of my career, having done everything else, I personally saw mainly equine patients. After the novelty of treating "all creatures, great and small," the horse remained my favorite patient.

My clientele included some of the best animal trainers in the world. Not only were there dog and horse trainers who were well known in the entertainment industry, but also a great assortment of wild animal

*I am here with one of my early patients, a young chimpan-
zee. They are cute when they are young.*

trainers. I learned a lot from these people. From some I learned how to
obtain incredible behavior from animals. And, from some I learned what
not to do. All of this background served to enhance my interest in animal
behavior. I have always read everything possible on the subject and attend
any and all presentations on behavior at scientific meetings.

During the first few years of my Conejo Valley practice, I saw a lot
of young apes, mostly chimpanzees and orangutans, along with a gorilla or
two. Since veterinary training back then did not include primates, I often
consulted with physicians about the problems I encountered.

Usually I consulted with pediatricians, but one case was different.
A baby chimp had been purchased from a pet shop by a couple. That was
common back then, before today's stringent regulations were in force. The
chimp seemed to be lame in one leg, so I X-rayed it. There was a buckshot

in the knee and two more elsewhere in the body. What probably happened was that the mother had been shot out of the trees for meat by natives. The baby, clinging to the mother, had survived the fall and its wounds. It was sold to a trader, managed to escape death due to disease or malnutrition, and ended up in a California pet shop.

I consulted with Lester Cohn, MD, an orthopedic surgeon, and together we operated successfully on the knee. Dr. Cohn took the full-body radiographs to the university hospital where he taught, and presented the case to his colleagues without mentioning that the patient was a chimpanzee. They were all horrified to see a baby with three buckshot in its body, but not one of them was aware that the baby was not human.

This brings me to the point of this chapter. Our closest relative in the animal world is the chimpanzee. Now, please, creationists, I'm not suggesting that we humans descended from chimps. But, we *do* have a common ancestor. We share 98 percent of the same DNA with chimpanzees. Biologically speaking we are one of the larger primates, and with them we share certain inherent traits. Unlike horses, in which the leader of the band is usually an older female, we large primates are usually led by a mature male. Rather than maintaining dominance by controlling

Chimpanzee patient in my early practice years.

the movement of his peers as does the alpha mare, the alpha primate rules by intimidation display and by what we would label "violence."

The first patient I treated at Pacific Ocean Park was a mature male chimp. He needed an injection and his two trainers were filled with dire warnings about how dangerous a mature male was. I was unconcerned because although I had only treated immature chimps, I thought they were cute. This male wasn't very large, either. He weighed 85 pounds. I weighed 155, one trainer was my size, and the other weighed 195 pounds.

One trainer, Tex, removed the chimp from the cage. Then, Wally, the other trainer, got behind the chimp and held him in a full Nelson wrestling hold. "Okay, Doc, we got him."

"This is just a simple little injection," I said, "there's no need for all this fuss."

I then injected the chimp's thigh.

Instantly, he grabbed both of my ankles with his *feet* and jerked me to the floor. "I got him," I laughed, "but, now he's got me!"

The explosion of rage that followed aborted my laughter. All four of us were down on the floor, the shrieking 85-pound chimp throwing both trainers from side to side. Now filled with apprehension I urged, "Don't let him go."

"We're trying, Doc. We're trying," they assured me. They finally wrestled the chimp over to his cage and got all of him but one arm in it. That arm clawed at me as he screamed in fury. He wanted *me*!

After he was finally caged, we all said, "Whew!"

"We told you he was tough, Doc!" the trainers said.

"If you had turned him loose," I asked, "do you think I could have bluffed him by standing my ground and shouting? I know that chimps use intimidation displays amongst themselves."

Wally Ross, a lifelong animal trainer who had literally worked with every conceivable species, spoke gravely. "Doc, if we'da turned him loose he would'a torn your face from your skull. That's what they do, you know. They tear your face off."

This was in 1959. I have feared mature chimps ever since and I have treated many of them. My face may not be beautiful, but I value it.

○ ○ ○

In 2005 an incident occurred at a private zoo near Bakersfield, California. Mr. and Mrs. James Davis visited the facility, which is an animal sanctuary, to visit a former pet that now resides there. According to the Associated Press newspaper stories, four chimps, two males and two females, escaped from their cages. While the two females fled the sanctuary, the two males attacked Mr. Davis. They tore off most of his face, one foot, and some fingers. And these were relatively young male chimps.

While I was the veterinarian for Pacific Ocean Park in 1959, the headline act of the summer was three divers from Acapulco, Mexico, whose finale was to dive off of a "100-foot tower" (which was actually 80 feet tall) into the dolphin pool.

Preceding this grand finale, three of my patients entertained the audience. They were three adolescent male chimps, all outfitted in cute little costumes. Throughout the summer, as the chimps came offstage, they passed the three divers in their resplendent swimsuits and capes. Then, one day late in the summer, as the trios passed each other, each chimp simultaneously attacked a diver, injuring all the men severely. I believe this was a planned attack.

I could write a book about chimp stories, rather than a chapter, but suffice it to say that many of the incidents I have witnessed or am familiar with, were horrific.

○ ○ ○

One of the privileges of a life spent working with animals—whether one is a farmer, rancher, zookeeper, zoologist, or veterinarian—is the insight such a career gives one into the roots of human behavior.

Observing so many species has helped me to understand territoriality, dominance hierarchy, male sexual aggressiveness, maternal nurturing instinct, and gender differences apparent in most species' behavior. The correlation in human behavior is all too apparent. A thin veneer of civilization separates us from other animals, and this veneer is applied to us early in life. Yet, despite the best parenting, optimum schooling, and moral and religious principles drilled into us from early childhood, we all revert at times to our primitive behavior. A glance at any newspaper is evidence that this happens all too often.

My veterinary practice included every conceivable species, including dolphins and whales.

When dealing with animals, humans instinctively resort to the behavior inherent in our species, especially if we are young and even more so if we are male. If we behave with horses in a chimpanzee-like manner, they will be intimidated. Horses stay alive by running away from anything they perceive to be dangerous. If unable to flee, they will fight. We humans must *alter* our natural species behavior to obtain that elusive goal with horses, an absolute lack of fear of us combined with total respect.

Two things can teach us how to behave in such a manner:

1. We can be taught. If we are *willing* to learn, the resources are readily available today. Schools, publications, the Internet, videos, and learning clinics all serve this purpose. Technology is the reason the revolution in horsemanship occurred now and not a century ago when our horse population was triple what it is now, despite a much smaller human population at that time.

2. We can use our unique human power of reason. It takes intelligence—a logical mind, an open mind, a receptive mind—to abandon any traditional technology that has (admittedly) served our purpose, in favor of a completely different approach.

Two kinds of behavior apply to horses and people. *Innate behavior,* coded in our DNA, is genetically predetermined, and unique to our species. In nature it is what helped the species to survive.

Learned behavior is enormously versatile. It allows creatures to do things that are of no practical survival value in nature, such as dogs catching Frisbees or singing on command, or horses spinning in a reining class or taking a bow, or a parakeet ringing a bell or saying "Hello." Learned behavior enables human beings to act "civilized" and not behave like the Paleolithic Stone Age creatures that we biologically are. Civility, courtesy, compromising, tolerance, and compassion are all learned behaviors. The *potential* for such behavior is present in every child, but it must be *taught*. It must be presented, encouraged, reinforced, and nurtured.

Mankind's first contact with animals was to hunt, kill, and eat them. We ate horses for countless millennia. For thousands of years after we domesticated horses, because we needed their speed, their strength, and their endurance, we primarily controlled them with coercive, forceful, and often brutal methods. After all, consider the behavioral traits that enabled men to hunt, pursue, and kill animals like the woolly mammoth, and the ancestors of today's cattle, hogs, and horses. We are *hunters!*

A few enlightened individuals could always put aside their predatory instincts and find a better way to communicate with horses, but they were exceptional. Most people depended upon coercion to control behavior, because the use of violence comes easily to most of mankind. Although we are specially endowed, we are still relatives of the chimpanzee.

We can be apish in our horsemanship, or, we can be enlightened. The choice is ours. Which provides greater pride?

CHAPTER SIXTEEN

Bigotry in the World of Horses

"Bigotry," as the dictionary defines it, is obstinate and blind attachment to a creed, opinion, or ritual.

It comes naturally to human beings. It's probably an expression of primitive tribalism and may have served to protect one Stone Age tribe's territory from infringement by another tribe. Bigotry, which exists in every aspect of human activity, is only overcome by teaching that it is harmful to a civilized society. It is not easily overcome because bigotry is a powerful emotion and because it makes us feel superior to the people or concepts against whom we are bigoted. Thus, we see bigotry of one race toward another or even all others, of one nation or state toward others, of the northern half of a state toward the southern half, of rural areas toward urban areas, of one school or one district of a community toward another, of neighbor toward neighbor, of one business, club, team, or chapter toward others. It is human nature.

You would think, for example, that those people that love boating would automatically share compatibility. Do you think that sailboat owners and powerboat owners all love each other? Are lovers of automobiles all compatible? Do the aficionados of antique cars, of sport cars, and of luxury cars all love and respect each other? Many people love to play in the snow, but do downhill skiers, snowboarders, cross country skiers, and snowmobilers all admire and encourage each other's choices?

So it is with horses. There is tremendous bigotry within the horse industry.

I once toured all over Argentina doing sixteen full-day seminars on equine behavior in thirty days. In Buenos Aires alone I did five, one for the polo club, one for the jockey club, one for the Arabian Horse Association, another for the Quarter Horse Association, and the last for the Criollo Horse people. Afterward, I asked my hosts why we had not simply done one for all five groups simultaneously.

"What?" I was told, "they won't even speak to each other."

In 1984, just prior to the Olympics in Los Angeles, I made a house call to a well-known dressage stable in western San Fernando Valley. Even though most of the horses boarded at the stable were dressage horses, a few local residents also boarded their trail riding horses there. My patient was a dumpy Arabian mare owned by a nice, petite older woman. She adored her little horse and rode her several times a week.

When I arrived at the stable, the manager introduced me to a gentleman from Europe who was there to coach the U.S. Olympic Equestrian Team.

"So, doctor, what are you here for?" the continental horseman asked.

"Just to worm and vaccinate a mare," I responded.

He nodded with approval, and we talked for a while until I saw a horse being led toward me. "Well," I said, "here comes my patient."

Smiling, my companion looked behind him and then said with disgust, "An Arabian!" He spat loudly upon the ground, "*Ptooey*! I *hate* them."

I instantly lost all respect for that man. He may have been a skilled horseman, but his bigoted remark was not that of a lover of horses.

Throughout my long career as an equine practitioner in southern California, I have seen many similar exhibitions of bigotry; English versus Western, classical versus non-classical, one breed versus another or, frequently, against *all* others.

I occasionally found people who owned several different breeds of horses. I recall a woman who owned a Quarter Horse, an Arabian, a Peruvian Paso, and an American Paint. The week before I wrote this chapter (indeed, they inspired it) I visited a man and his wife who owned, on small acreage, three Clydesdales, a Gypsy Vanner mare, a BLM-adopted mustang, a couple of BLM-adopted donkeys and their offspring, a mule, and a Quarter Horse. People like these are Horse Lovers!

This isn't to suggest that those who own horses of a single breed aren't also horse lovers, not at all. But those who own a variety of horses are definitely horse lovers, whereas those who own a single breed *may* be horse lovers, but they may also be in the horse business for other reasons that I will address shortly.

First, however, let me say that as a mule owner, breeder, and trainer, I have been made keenly aware of equine bigotry by comments heard when people learn of my involvement with mules. Certainly the most extreme example I can give is when a man asked, "Mules? What do you do with them?" I explained that we ride them and that we do all the things on them that people do with horses.

His response has to be a classic definition of bigotry: "Only [that offensive *N* word] ride mules!"

My contempt can only be imagined.

It should be noted here that *all* mule lovers are horse lovers, but by no means are *all* horse lovers also mule lovers. The reason is that many people are involved with horses because they are role playing. Some people go for English horses not because they like to jump, or because of the technology of English horsemanship, but because they feel that it is sophisticated, or socially elite, or suggestive of British upper class.

Similarly, some people are attracted to dressage not because of the intimate communication it demands, but because it is "continental" or makes them feel that they are members of nobility. The same emotion attracts other people to Saddlebreds, or Arabians, or other breeds.

Even Western horsepeople are not exempt from this motivation. Some are not role playing Roy Rogers, or John Wayne, or even a working cowboy, but rather a cattle baron. Sometimes, if they own more than one acre—even just an acre and a half—they like to name their place Cactus Acres, or Green Acres, or Blankety-blank Farms, using the plural. And, of course, in the Western states, *any* piece of land with a horse on it is now a "ranch." The term "ranch" is so often misused, especially in California, that it has lost all meaning.

A *farm* is an agricultural entity wherein the soil is tilled, planted, and harvested. A *ranch* is an agricultural entity wherein natural forage is grazed. Therefore, although a *farm* may occupy many thousands of acres, a *ranch*, on the other hand (like mine), may consist of just a few acres, but the grass growing on those acres is grazed.

Chicken "ranches," asparagus "ranches," and almond "ranches" aren't ranches at all. They are "farms" or "orchards," but it makes many people feel better to think they own a "ranch."

I first became aware of role playing within the horse world when I moved to California from Arizona in 1957. I attended my first polo match, and afterwards, many people gathered in the clubhouse to drink and socialize. Many of them (not the players, but the groupies) were speaking like Englishmen. "Good show, Reggie." "Well done, Gordon!" "Pity, Christopher!"

I slowly realized that these people were speaking and acting in an unnatural manner, probably in a way gleaned from motion pictures.

After all, the overwhelming majority of Americans come from very common stock. We are the descendants of penniless immigrants, struggling pioneers, crude frontiersmen, vagrants, rootless wanderers, slaves, Stone Age natives, European military deserters, and shipwrecked sailors . . . with notable aristocratic exceptions, of course.

The single greatest virtue of America is freedom, including the freedom to better oneself in the absence of the Old World's rigid traditions, class distinctions, and snobbishness. So, why do we assume the role of Old World nobility? Conversely, many Americans are proud of being "the Common Man." I suppose that many of us mule fanciers take pride in owning and riding a hybrid, crossbred creature with an (undeserved) reputation for cussedness and a powerful work ethic.

I made a call once to worm and vaccinate several horses at a luxurious rural estate. I had not been there before, and when I rang the doorbell it was answered by a young woman. Behind her I could see two children, not quite of school age.

"Yes?" she asked sweetly.

"I'm Doctor Miller," I explained.

"Oh!" She smiled and said brightly and softly, "I'll be right out, just as soon as I change my clothes. The horses are all ready for you."

A few minutes later she emerged dressed in boots and an old stained cowboy hat. She spat upon the ground, hitched up her jeans, and loudly said, "Okay, let's go do these suckers!"

Role playing!

One of my clients, years ago, was a young psychiatrist. The first time I was called to his place he met me dressed in a big Western hat, bat-wing chaps, and big roweled spurs. I assumed that he had been trail riding or was planning to do so. However, on subsequent visits he was always dressed this way. Then, he finally explained to me that horses were his perfect escape from a very stressful profession. "That's why I dress this way," he explained. "I'm role playing. It's part of my escape routine."

Sadly, some people are involved with horses for less creative reasons. There are people who experience "mastery" by controlling a large and powerful beast. Some of these people can be cruel in their handling of horses.

Most people who go into the horse business to make money find great disappointment. There are few who make enough money to compensate for the investment they have to make—the risk, the labor, and the necessary working hours. Frankly, that includes my own profession. Veterinarians average more than eight years of higher education, usually at enormous expense, then obligate themselves to a huge investment in their practice facilities and a stressfully demanding career. They can only be compared to a country physician, with the added disadvantage of often dangerous patients. They earn surprisingly little. The average income, despite long hours under arduous conditions, is well below that of physicians, dentists, or attorneys. Yet, and I say this with gratitude and pride, doctors of veterinary medicine are overwhelmingly the happiest of all professionals.

After considering all the role playing, the expense in owning horses, the emotional attachment we develop toward these animals, and the time we must devote to them, it isn't surprising that the devotees of the various equestrian disciplines often display intolerance or at least indifference to other disciplines.

Racehorse people are often completely indifferent to any other kind of horse or horsemanship. It is "the sport of kings," and some owners and trainers look down on all other horses and horse activities. English and dressage people often disparage Western riders or other kinds of horsemanship. Once at an Arabian horse farm that competed very successfully in Western and

English show classes, I spied a sixteen-hand filly with the head of a classical Arabian and the body of Secretariat. "Wow!" I said. "What's this?"

"Oh," the owner replied, "she's a mutant. A freak! She's a two-year-old and we can't get rid of her. Nobody wants her."

Alexandra Dees is a breeder of Lusitano horses in Ventura County, California, where I reside. Trained for such different disciplines as dressage, reining, roping, and cutting, neither her horses nor their owner suffers from a bigoted view of horsemanship. Here her stallion does it all.

The Lusitano stallion Pincelin cutting bison.

Pincelin performing dressage with Alfredo Hernandez up.

Eric Youngblood heels a heifer on Pincelin.

Pincelin as a working cowhorse.

I knew that such "mutants" were the origin of the Thoroughbred breed. After admiring her conformation I asked if I could watch her move. The owner, hoping that I could find a gullible would-be Arabian breeder to buy her, gladly longed her for me. The filly moved like a dream with a natural dwell in her gaits, and elevation. "I think you have a great dressage prospect here," I told the owners.

"Dressage? We don't do dressage."

"Well," I said, "tonight I'll call some of my dressage clients and see if somebody is interested in her."

After work, I called all of my best dressage trainer clients and told them that I knew of an outstanding filly that was available very cheaply.

Every conversation went the same way after I described the filly:

"She sounds fantastic, Doc. What's her breeding?"

My answer, "She's a purebred Arabian," resulted in disappointed silence.

Not one of those trainers would even go out to look at the extraordinary filly. Eventually, she sold very cheaply to a wanna-be breeder.

Blind bigotry!

Over the course of my career most of the Western horsepeople I have known have viewed classical horsemen with contempt. There have been notable exceptions, and their open-mindedness has served to contribute mightily to their horsemanship skills. Jimmy Williams, recognized as one of California's greatest horsemen, was such a person. Monte Foreman, the pioneering Western horseman of the mid-twentieth century, was another. But, such people were rare.

Now, however, we are in this great revolution in horsemanship, and, for the first time, an increasing number of influential horsemen are blending the best of the various disciplines. Natural horsemanship clinicians like Pat Parelli and Dennis Reis, from cowboy backgrounds and who use Western saddles and tack, are increasingly seen performing and advocating dressage techniques.

Conversely, a lifelong dressage competitor in Norway told me that she rides every day, and when she rides for pleasure she now prefers to ride Western. When I asked her why, she responded, "When I ride for pleasure I can now ride with a loose rein, using one hand, the other hand free. I am relaxed, and my horse is relaxed." Then she added a perspective I had never considered. "After all, dressage is from a military origin, and Western riding from a pastoral origin."

○ ○ ○

In the next two chapters I will relate the stories of two remarkable men who, from radically different backgrounds, have managed to combine the disciplines of Western and classical European horsemanship, and ended up in much the same place. Their life stories are intriguing and touching. Most important, what they have achieved forecasts that the traditional bigotry within the horse world, which has limited the ancient art and science of horsemanship, is going to end. There is a light at the end of the tunnel, and both horses and the people involved with them will benefit.

CHAPTER SEVENTEEN

A Boyhood Dream Fulfilled

Eitan Beth-Halachmy was born in 1940 in the small town of Rishon-Lezion in what is now the state of Israel. Riding by age five, Eitan had a great love for horses early on. When he was thirteen, he attended an agricultural boarding school, and spent a lot of time working the fields with horses and mules, riding them home after work, and pleasure riding in his spare time. The school bred, raised, and trained their own horses and mules.

While a student at the school, he saw his first American western movie and immediately decided that he would become an American cowboy when he grew up. Like millions of other boys, his hero was Roy Rogers, but unlike most of them, Eitan's dream became a reality.

He spent two years at the Israeli government national stud farm. He became assistant manager, exercised the stallions, and maintained the

A portrait.

barn. He learned a lot from the farm's general manager, George Adam, a former Yugoslavian cavalry officer. From him Eitan learned about classical horsemanship and equine behavior. He was also influenced by a Hungarian ex-circus trainer named Leopold. At eighteen years of age he entered the armed forces, as do all Israeli youth, both male and female. He served for three years as a paratrooper.

In 1961, he came to the United States for the first time as an International Farm Youth exchange student, spending that year on farms and ranches in West Virginia, Minnesota, and California. All of the families that he stayed with owned horses. He began riding Western and knew that he wanted someday to return to the United States and realize his boyhood dream.

The next year he entered the University of Vienna as a pre-veterinary student. He worked at the Spanish Riding School as a stall cleaner for the next three years. He was, as he says, "a sponge," asking questions and observing and learning all he could. He learned "patience," and the importance of "the partnership between horse and rider." From the Spanish Riding School's staff of lifetime grooms he learned "how important the work ethic is to horses."

In 1968, he immigrated to the United States, where he would stay permanently. He attended the University of California at Davis studying animal science and plant pathology. He rode horses for others at every opportunity and pursued his talents as a sculptor and artist. He believes that being an artist gives one "an edge in life," that creativity allows one to "dream beyond traditional boundaries" and maintain a positive attitude, which, he says, is very important if one is involved with horses.

Living in Davis, he worked in gas stations when "gas was 28 cents a gallon and service was part of the job." He sold some artwork and invented a chlorination system for swimming pools. He built a four-wheel-drive car with two engines, one in front and one in back.

In 1984, he began training horses for the public. He trained and showed all breeds, including ponies, mules, and warmbloods, but mostly Quarter Horses. From Davis he moved to Sonoma, training Quarter Horses, and then in 1985 he moved to Grass Valley in the western foothills of the Sierra Nevada mountains, where he has been ever since. One of his clients purchased a Morgan horse and brought it to his barn to be trained.

The Morgan became a favorite breed. He met Debbie, an American woman who also was a Morgan owner, and they married.

Eitan's accomplishments have become legendary, especially within the Morgan breed. He has for many years won multiple titles including Outstanding Morgan Showman. He has also won the World's Championship in the open division in reining and Western pleasure. A popular clinician, he is also known to many people because of the spectacular performances at many expositions and other horse related events that he calls cowboy dressage.

Cowboy dressage is classical European horsemanship, but it is done with Western tack; both horse and rider are "dressed western." The horsemanship is classical, but it is done on a loose rein or what Eitan calls a "draped rein," and in a very relaxed manner. His cues are so subtle as to be virtually invisible to the average observer. Many horse owners, inspired by his expertise, want him to teach them his methods. He tells them, "I cannot teach you to do what I do, but I can help you to become the best rider that you can be."

This incredibly talented man says he has learned by observing others, reading many books, studying a lot of videos, and spending a

Cowboy dressage.

The classical California headset.

lifetime in the saddle, but mostly from living with horses. "They taught me more than anyone or anything else. In more recent years, teaching and giving clinics, I learned a lot from my students and their needs. Their questions made me think harder and seek answers." He maintains that the differences between Western and classical horsemanship are superficial: "We are all dealing with the same animal."

If horsemanship is both an art and a science, Eitan is an artist. An extremely talented videographer, his cowboy dressage videos, produced by Debbie and him at their Wolf Creek Ranch, in Grass Valley, California, are masterpieces. Viewing them, many people are moved to tears by the overwhelming beauty of the music, the scenery, and the magnificent horses and horsemanship.

In September 2006 Eitan was invited to do his cowboy dressage at the World Equestrian Games in Aachen, Germany. His performance brought an audience of 60,000 to their feet. The Western saddle and his cowboy hat notwithstanding, the crowd appreciated the spectacular

Eitan at the 2006 World Equestrian Games in Aachen, Germany.

horsemanship that they saw. At sixty-six years of age Eitan finally gained world recognition.

Isn't it fascinating that this man, whose background has been in classical European horsemanship, is now one of the best Western horsemen in the world?

How different his background is from that of Lester Buckley (described in the next chapter), but you will observe how they have arrived at a similar destination. Perhaps it was inevitable. Both share a consuming passion for the horse. Both have that rare combination of physical and mental attributes that are the hallmarks of great horsemen. Each has the physical dexterity, the balance, the swift reaction time, the observant senses, the empathy, the patience, the sensitivity, the kindness, and the gentleness that are necessary traits of the finest horsemen. Each of them has remarkable hands.

CHAPTER EIGHTEEN

For the Love of a Horse

Like Eitan Beth-Halachmy, who had his future shaped by seeing western movies as a boy, Lester Buckley was similarly influenced, but his background is as radically different from Eitan's as is possible—culturally, historically, and geographically.

Lester was born in Lovington, New Mexico. His parents moved to a small ranch in Desdemona, Texas, soon after his birth. Orphaned at six years of age, he was raised by his aunt and uncle who adopted him. They, too, owned a small Texas ranch, so Lester grew up in an agricultural environment.

When Lester was eight years of age, his family took him to Forth Worth, Texas, to see the Spanish Riding School, which was on a tour of the United States. Mesmerized, the boy thought, "Someday I want to be able to do things like that with horses." Like Eitan, he has been able to realize that boyhood dream. His love for one horse made it happen.

Lester attended Sul Ross University, a popular school for Texas ranch kids and one that has always had a great intercollegiate rodeo team. While a student at Sul Ross, Lester went to a Ray Hunt horsemanship clinic. Inspired, he made a decision: "This is what I want to do with the rest of my life." He attended as many clinics as he could that were conducted by Ray Hunt and other natural horsemanship clinicians and studied their methods.

After graduating from college, he went to work starting colts and introducing them to cattle for Rex Caubles' Cutter Bill Ranch in Denton, Texas. He then worked for an outfitter who had a pack station in western Canada and who wintered in Texas. Lester started colts for him, most of them five- to ten-year-olds that had run wild all of their lives. Worked in a round pen made of logs, unbroken horses of this age, which had run wild in a wolf-infested country, were the ultimate challenge for a colt starter. The experience served him well.

Lester apprenticed for the next seven years with cutting horse trainer Willy Richardson in Texas and New Mexico. During this time he started showing cutting horses and he also continued to attend Ray Hunt clinics.

He and a college friend, Jimmy Scudday, went to work for the King Ranch in Texas where they started large numbers of colts, using natural horsemanship methods. This job occupied them for several months of the year, after which they would go to Hawaii to start colts for the famous Parker Ranch.

Both the King Ranch and the Parker Ranch, huge traditional cattle ranches, had always started their own colts. However, the revolution in horsemanship had begun, and like other large ranches, they were now hiring professional colt starters experienced in gentler modern techniques rather than the old "bronc bustin'" methods.

After three years of working together, Scudday got married and Lester continued training on his own. Lester had worked for the Parker Ranch for four years starting colts when he was seriously hurt. He had started more than seventy colts that year when a filly—during her first ride—fell with him and was cast under a fence. Lester was pinned under her while she thrashed and struggled. He was all alone, and it was late in the evening. Fortunately, somebody who came by to visit was able to help him get free. He had severe injuries including a dislocated hip. Infection set in and doctors thought he would have to have an arm amputated. However, thanks to antibiotics, Lester's arm was saved.

After Lester got out of the hospital, he took the next winter off building fences, and not doing much horse training. The next year he returned to the Parker Ranch as horse herd foreman. The ranch was running more than six hundred head of horses at that time, and Lester was in charge of all breeding and training.

I met Lester while he was in Hawaii. Recognizing his extraordinary horsemanship skills, I proposed that we do some clinics together. This was the beginning of a long-term relationship. Just as I had recognized the genius of Pat Parelli when he was in his mid-twenties, I am very proud that I saw Lester Buckley's remarkable talent and his gift for horsemanship the first time I saw him ride. I don't share such skills, but I do recognize them when I see them, and I understand them.

Lester returned to Texas to become a successful cutting horse trainer, working primarily with American Paint Horses. He did so for several years, winning such titles as Superstakes Reserve Champion Paint Cutting Horse and also the Top Ten Honor Roll.

In 2001, Lester called me. He explained that his own great cutting horse, Colonel Win, was fourteen years of age and completely sound of wind and limb. However, the horse was going blind. He said, "He has cataracts and I want you to tell me who is the best veterinary eye surgeon in the world. This horse means a lot to me and I'll fly him to Europe if necessary to have a cataract operation."

Lester Buckley cutting when he was a trainer in Texas.

I telephoned five board-certified veterinary ophthalmologists. All five told me that Texas A & M University had the necessary personnel, experience, and equipment to perform the operations. Lester took Colonel Win to the university and had an operation done on the more severely affected eye. Unfortunately, as happens sometimes, the surgery failed. The eye was lost.

Shortly afterward, in 2003, Lester moved back to Hawaii, flying Colonel Win, his beloved horse there, too. He then phoned me again. "My horse has only one eye and he's going blind in that one. He's still sound and he loves to work. I can't cut on him, I can't rein on him, I can't rope on him, but I figured out something he can do."

"What's that?" I asked.

"He can do dressage."

"Lester," I said, "you have a one-eyed horse that's going blind in his remaining eye and you're going to sell him as a *dressage horse*?"

"Sell him?" Lester protested. "Hell, no, I'll *never* sell this horse. I love him. I'm going to learn dressage!"

"Really?" I responded, trying to picture this Texas cowboy in dressage attire. "Where are you going to learn dressage, in Hawaii?"

Former cutting horse Colonel Win, now blind, teaches children to ride.

"No! I signed up for lessons in Germany. I asked several people, and they said that the schools in Vechta and Warendorf in Germany were the best places for me to learn, so I'm going to Vechta for two weeks next year."

After moving back to Hawaii, Lester married Mary, a lovely widow whose husband had died in a boating accident. Mary went to Germany with him and reported that people snickered when Lester showed up in his cowboy hat and jeans. However, when a breeding farm owner saw him ride, he said, "You have the best hands I have ever seen." You see, a horseman is a horseman, in any land, wearing any hat, and on any horse.

Toward the end of the two-week course, somebody was trying to load an unruly, reluctant big warmblood into a van. The usual battle ensued. After a while, Lester, who is a quiet man, asked if he could be of assistance. Within twenty minutes Lester had the big horse willingly and passively loading and unloading on command. Afterward, he was asked by the instructor whether he intended to return the following year. He said yes, that he had signed up for another two-week dressage course. "Can you stay an extra two weeks?" the instructor asked. "We'd like you to conduct a course in horsemanship on the ground."

Lester Buckley jumping.

In 2006, Lester was again a dressage student in Germany. He also taught both ground school, problem solving, and Western horsemanship. He has been awarded class three and class four performance medals in both dressage and jumping by the German FN (Fédération Equestre Nationale). In 2007, Texas cowboy Lester Buckley was awarded his international trainer/instructor license.

When true horsemen see colleagues from other disciplines and other cultures, they do not reject what they see. Instead, they seize the opportunity to learn and expand their own knowledge. Heinrich Ramsbock, one of the largest and most successful breeders of sport horses in Europe, bought a Western stallion and tack and learned natural horsemanship. Lester's and Ramsbock's trainers are teaching each other. The school at Vechta is adding Western horsemanship to its curriculum.

At Lester's clinic in January of 2006, a visiting judge of combined training (dressage and jumping) said in English: "What you are doing is outstanding. We needed this. We will look forward to your return."

Back in Hawaii, Lester has now imported warmbloods, and he and Mary have a breeding operation in Germany. Colonel Win is now retired

Lester Buckley on a warmblood.

Lester Buckley riding dressage.

and is teaching children the basics of dressage. He is pastured together with Esquire, a Hanoverian gelding, and they are inseparable.

Lester Buckley is a younger man than Eitan Beth-Halachmy. In the years ahead, I am confident that the horse world will recognize his talent and his dedication. Like Eitan, he has the imagination and a mind open to new concepts. These are horsemen not locked into tradition. They are above the bigotry and small-mindedness that restrict so many people in their life's work. They are leaders in this revolution in horsemanship that is improving the lives of both horses and the people who work with them. They are breaking down the wall that has separated the horsemanship disciplines.

How many other human endeavors would benefit by such open-mindedness?

CHAPTER NINETEEN

Look at Their Hands

The great nineteenth-century expert, Dennis Magner, said that "to be a good horseman, one must have the delicacy of touch and feeling of a woman, the courage of a lion, and the hang-on pluck of a bulldog." Another way of expressing the same concept is to say that "the ideal horseman has the courage of a lion, the patience of a saint, and the hands of a woman."

Why is this so?

The lion unhesitatingly attacks prey many times his size. For a lion to pounce upon a Cape buffalo, one of the most aggressive of all grazing animals, takes great courage that is motivated by a fierce hunger. Similarly, humans, working with horses which outweigh them tremendously, in order to obtain their compliance, must have courage.

Without patience, our ability to effectively communicate with horses is severely compromised. This is especially true because most horsemen are highly competitive. Indeed, it is competition that is the reason so many of us enjoy working with horses. That sense of competition takes a great variety of forms ranging from relatively placid Western pleasure show classes to rigorous endurance racing, from intricate dressage to extremely active cross-country eventing or barrel racing. Yet, even the most compulsive competitor must learn patience if he or she is to work most effectively with the horse.

Finally, the hands of a woman. Should a team roper, a fox hunter, or a team penner have the "hands of a woman?" What does that mean?

We humans are unique among primates in having an opposable thumb that facilitates the use of tools. The most basic of all human tools is the club. The fist, tightly closed, securely grasps the club, the opposable thumb locking it in place, creating, in effect, a greatly extended arm. By swinging a club, this extension combined with centrifugal force gave primitive man a formidable weapon. The closed fist, therefore, is mankind's primary defense. Not our teeth as in a dog, nor our head as in cattle, nor flight as in a horse, but our closed fist.

In primitive societies, using tools, the men did most of the hunting and defense of the group. Thus, the closed fist is a masculine stance. Conversely, the opened fingers is a feminine stance. Observe the hands of men and women. A hand that is dorsiflexed—that is, bent upwards at the wrist, the fingers open to a greater or lesser degree, is seen as "feminine." A wrist that is flexed ventrally (downward) with the fingers more or less closed to form a fist, is seen as "masculine."

Until recent times, horsemanship was an exclusively male domain. Most schools of horsemanship taught that reins should be held with a closed hand, the natural position for the male of our species. However, if we seek the ultimate degree of lightness in a horse, the closed hand is incompatible with that goal.

Our *fingers* are the most delicately innervated part of our anatomy. They have the richest nerve supply, and are the most sensitive parts of our arms. If we communicate with the most sensitive part of a horse—its mouth—with the most sensitive part of *our* body, we must use our fingers. Although so many schools of horsemanship, both past and present, have taught us to use the closed hand, and despite that so many continue to do so, the finest horsemen, past and present, do not handle the reins that way.

Have you ever meant to turn a single page of something you were reading and picked up two pages by mistake? Or, perhaps, you try to pick up a single sheet of paper, but got two? Isn't it remarkable, considering how thin a sheet of paper is, that our fingers instantly detect the excessive thickness of two sheets? Even if the fingers are the calloused digits of a full-time horseman? The incredibly delicate nerve endings in our finger tips can *feel* the difference.

The mouth of the horse, a grazing animal that must constantly differentiate between palatable and undesirable vegetation, is similarly innervated.

This is why we say that the ultimate tactile communication between horse and human involves the mouth of the horse and the *fingertips* of the human. If we use the closed fist to hold the reins, what must the horse suffer? Of course, fingertip control of the horse requires a highly trained, *responsive* horse, which is what natural horsemanship encourages.

There is currently a fad for bitless bridles. They work—most proponents of natural horsemanship start colts in simple halters. But bitless bridles are not the optimum way to communicate with the horse. Skillful fingers, delicately handling reins attached to a bit, are the most effective and humane means of communication between horse and rider.

Are the advocates of bitless bridles correct when they say that the bit is a cruel instrument? Unfortunately, many riders misuse the bit. Go watch a John Wayne movie if you want to see a coarse and inhumane use of the bit.

When I was in my early twenties, I was riding a green colt on a summer ranch job. An eighty-year-old cowboy criticized me. "Boy! You hold those reins like they are made of barbed wire. Take a hold of them or that colt is going to take his head away from you and buck you off."

That old man had learned coercive horsemanship. It was the only way he knew. In the photographs accompanying this chapter are men—very masculine men—but *look at their hands*. These are the hands of men who both emotionally and physically have tremendous feelings for the horse. They are consumed with desire, not to *conquer* the horse, but to *communicate* with him. This is best done with the fingers, not with the closed hand.

The hands of a great horseman. This is Eitan Beth-Halachmy of Grass Valley, California.

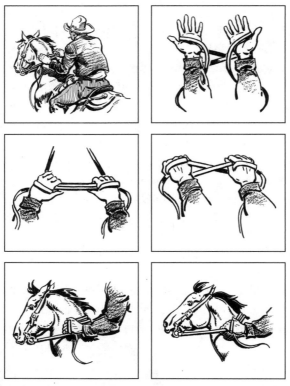

Since its inception, Western Horseman *magazine, published in Colorado Springs, Colorado, has chronicled the advancement of Western Horsemanship. This illustration by Joe de Yong (* Western Horseman, *June 1949, "Tricks of a Rough, Tough Trade") shows a suggested method of handling green colts. Any reader of this magazine today, over half a century later, will note the very different methods now being used to start colts; which attest to the success of "The Revolution in Horsemanship."*

Martin Black, a great Idaho clinician, on a mature bronc that he saddled five minutes earlier for the first time. Look at his hands.

Eitan Beth-Halachmy

Jon Ensign, Montana clinician, working a green colt on the ground. Soft hands, even at this early stage.

The hands of Lester Buckley, the subject of the previous chapter.

Here I am, on the first ride on a mule colt. Look at my hands.

California clincian Rod Bergen demonstrates to trainees at the Los Angeles Sheriff's Department Mounted Unit his "one finger hold" on a lead rope. See Chapter 23 for more about police horses.

It is easy for most women to "have the hands of a woman." This is Harley McCluskey riding a zebra, Spots 'n Stripes Zurprise. She is a student of trainer/clinician Nancy Nunke in Ramona, California's Spots 'n Stripes Ranch. The ranch uses natural horsemanship methods on its 30 zebras.

CHAPTER TWENTY

Skeptics

Now that the revolution in horsemanship is firmly established and is rapidly spreading, skeptical objections from many traditional horsemen are heard less often. However, during the first two decades after Ray Hunt launched his first clinics, which were followed and emulated by other "converted cowboys," frequent denials were expressed by people who had both pride and confidence in their own successful traditional methods.

Seeing a colt worked in a round pen, mounted, and ridden in half an hour or less without the use of force and without the horse bucking was something many trainers could not accept because *they* couldn't do it. Similarly, seeing so-called outlaw horses with reputations for all sorts of violent and antisocial behavior completely changed in a remarkably short time caused scoffers to cry, "fake!" Most commonly, such skeptics accused clinicians of using drugs to subdue the horse or claimed that the clinician had secretly worked with the horse prior to the clinic.

Such accusations were not new. In ancient times the spectacular results obtained by great horsemen were often explained as their being in league with the devil or the result of witchcraft. Ignorant people have always explained many scientific phenomena by resorting to mysticism.

Kell B. Jeffery, the enlightened Australian horseman, spent his twentieth-century lifetime trying to teach people to convert to his methods, which he called a "New Deal for Horses." Although largely unsuccessful because the historical moment for the horse world to accept and support a revolution had not yet arrived, he did manage to win a number of followers in his home country. One of these was a man named Des Kirk, who in a manual titled *Horse Breaking Made Easy* begins with a tribute to his mentor that relates an incident that occurred at a demonstration in 1953. A large crowd watched Jeffery change a difficult horse with ease:

"At lunch time people were asking each other how in the world he could have drugged that horse to make him go so quietly," writes Kirk. "The Jeffery method was so effective that people could not believe their own eyes."

In 1997, BBC Television asked me to narrate a film that showed the taming of a wild mustang by clinician Monty Roberts. The film is a dramatic and beautiful example of how a captured and unbroken wild horse can be converted to a safe and gentle mount in a remarkably short time. For years afterward, people who knew me and had seen the documentary wanted to know what *really* happened.

I was asked questions like: "I heard that the horse was tranquilized. What was he given?" or "I heard that the horse was fourteen years old and was purchased from a rodeo contractor. Is that true?" or "I was told that Monty spent weeks working with the horse before the film was made. Did he?" Most amazing was the question from a fellow veterinarian who knew me well:

"I heard there was a vet present who tranquilized the horse. Who did it?"

My response was, "*I* was the vet, and the horse was given nothing!"

To all of the dubious inquiries I would respond, "Your question indicates a belief that an unhandled wild horse *cannot* be gentled and tamed in a few hours using appropriate, scientifically sound psychological means. I was doing this myself in my twenties. It's easily explained and anybody can learn to do it, *but only if he or she believes that it can be done!*"

Several people have said to me, "You know Pat Parelli and you have worked with him. What kind of dope do you give those colts before he starts them?" These people assume that, because *they* can't do something, it cannot be done, an attitude that immediately causes a closed mind. A mind that is closed to anything new *cannot* learn. Obviously, this applies not only to horsemanship, but to any other kind of learning. To become proficient at *anything*, we must *want* to learn.

Interestingly, Monty Roberts made a sequel to his mustang documentary a year later. In it, the colt, now named Shy Boy, is used to gather cattle on a California roundup, then turned loose to see if he'll go back to Nevada where he was born and was captured by the Bureau of Land Management the previous year. After fraternizing with a domestic herd, he voluntarily returns to Monty. The dozens of people present, including Monty and me, were surprised and delighted when Shy Boy worked his way down the mountain and went right up to the man who had started him a year earlier.

It was a great moment but, again, the questions: "That wasn't the same horse, was it?"

"Was he starved so he'd come back for food?" "Was he deprived of water so he'd come back?" "What did you do, addict him to a narcotic?"

Pat Parelli made a *National Geographic* TV program in which he and his crew rounded up a band of New Mexico's mustangs so that their DNA could be tested in a study to determine their ancestry. These were previously unhandled, completely wild horses. Using the round pen and natural horsemanship, Parelli was standing on one filly's back in forty minutes.

The skeptical comments this elicited would have been hilarious if they weren't so pathetic. Rather than responding with "I want to learn how to do that," too many people responded with, "Fake! It can't be done!"

An annual colt-starting competition called Road to the Horse has been held for several years now. Three or four prominent clinicians, all experts in natural horsemanship methods, are each given an unbroken colt and allowed three hours to start it. At the end of the second day, they must demonstrate what they have accomplished.

In 2005, Clinton Anderson won the competition, standing on his colt's back, firing twelve rounds from two revolvers, cracking a stock whip, and starting up a chain saw and a leaf blower.

I was one of the five judges for the event, but the only veterinarian. Afterwards, I was asked: "What kind of tranquilizer was used?" "Did you supply Clinton with a tranquilizer and was it available to the other contestants?" "That horse was numb. Was it hypnotized or drugged?"

Obviously, the questioners could not accept the reality of natural horsemanship.

Everything is a mystery until it is explained scientifically. There is far more unknown to us than is known, but we are learning more all the time about ourselves, our world, our universe, and existence. The key to learning is a thirst for knowledge. The success of the revolution in horsemanship is but a small step in the advancement of civilization, but it is an important step.

After six thousand years of handling horses primarily with means natural to us, we are learning to use means of communication that are natural to the horse.

CHAPTER TWENTY-ONE

The Working Horse

Born eighty years ago, I am old enough to remember the last days of the working horse. Although automobiles, trucks, and motorcycles had largely replaced horses in the city streets, the clop, clop of the milkman's delivery-wagon horse was still serving as the morning alarm clock. Junk wagons and vegetable and fruit vendor wagons were still pulled by horses.

On the farm, despite the availability of tractors, horses were still in widespread use. During those Great Depression and Dust Bowl days, many farmers could scarcely afford a tractor. Combines were still being pulled by huge teams of horses or mules, and the cotton mule was an everyday sight in the deep South.

After the attack upon Pearl Harbor on December 7, 1941, the United States belatedly entered World War II. The prodigious war being fought in Europe, Africa, and the Pacific required all possible fuel supplies. This resulted in a temporary resurgence of the horse both in the city and the country. Early in the war my Boy Scout troop collected scrap metal for the war effort using a rented team and wagon. I proudly drove the team. Summers, in 1942 and 1943, I worked as a war effort farmhand for a dollar a day, much of the time driving a team and wagon, or walking behind a single horse-drawn cultivator. The best part of the day was riding the horses home in the evening. I even did some logging using horses. I never dreamed, at sixteen years of age, that the war would last long enough for me to serve in it as a soldier.

When the war ended in 1945, the displacement of the working horse in both cities and farms renewed rapidly. Summer ranch jobs allowed me to continue working with horses after I left the army and began a college career that ended nine years later when I graduated as a doctor of veterinary medicine.

Horse trailers were a rarity in the forties. Nowadays it is common to haul ranch horses to their work site by truck and trailer. Back then we'd ride from the ranch headquarters, often many miles, to where we would work cattle, and then ride the same distance back at the end of the day. Although horse trailers were rare and usually crude homemade affairs, it was common to fit a rack on the back of a pickup truck, and horses were trained to jump up into the bed of the truck. It amuses me today to see trailers, usually in foreign lands or in the Eastern United States, fitted with ramps because people don't think a horse can be trained to step up into a trailer lacking a ramp.

Ranch horses were tough then. Not broke until at least four years of age, they commonly were still working hard in their twenties. And, the men riding them were often in their seventies or eighties, which means that some of them had been riding in the post–Civil War golden era of the cowboy.

When I graduated veterinary school in 1956, the domestic horse population in the United States had dropped to slightly more than two million. That was one tenth of what it had been in 1910. Most of those two million were still actual working horses. It seemed to me at the time that the only way I could do equine practice was at the racetrack, or in cattle ranching country. The racetrack did not appeal to me. I decided while still in college to locate in an area of cattle ranching.

I don't think anybody foresaw the resurgence of the horse to its present American population of more than nine million. Of course, these are nearly all recreational horses. In the category of "recreational" I include racehorses, rodeo horses, cutting horses, sport horses, hunters, jumpers, urban cart horses, guest ranch mounts, and the millions of family "backyard" horses and ponies. Yes, they all work, often very hard, but their *purpose* is still recreational.

The number of actual working horses continues to fall. Many farmers, ranchers, and loggers use horses for their work, not because they *have* to, but because they *want* to do so. For this reason, the draft breeds are increasing in number, and for those of us who love horses, we are glad.

If a beer company uses teams to promote its product, that isn't what I refer to as a "working horse." They work, but what they do is elective. Machines can do it better and probably cheaper despite rising fuel prices. The Budweiser Clydesdales may not technically be regarded as "recreational," but as thrilling as they are to watch, I don't include them in this chapter, which is devoted to the working horse.

Even on the cattle ranches of Canada, the Western states, and America's Southeast, the numbers of horses, once considered *essential* to the operation, are diminishing. Mechanization continues to displace the horse except on those ranches that *prefer* to work from horseback for reasons of tradition, sentiment, or because the owners and the employees simply love to work with horses.

What has happened on Hawaii's huge, sprawling Parker Ranch foretells the future of the working horse on many, and perhaps most, of our cattle ranches.

I first visited the "Big Island" of Hawaii, the largest of the Hawaiian islands, forty years ago. At that time the ranch was running about 45,000

Dr. Doug Hammill, of East Glacier Park, Montana, is a retired veterinarian now engaged as a clinician specializing in draft and driving horses. Here he is logging with Tom, a 20-year-old Clydesdale gelding that wasn't started until 6 years of age.

head of cattle on the home ranch. Fifty to sixty cowboys worked these cattle from horseback. The horse herd on the ranch numbered between 2,500 and 3,000. This included a band of three hundred broodmares and a lot of unbroken horses, in addition to those used by the cowboys. It was not unusual for the men to ride out fifteen to twenty miles to work cattle, and then ride back again when the work was done.

I returned to the Big Island a decade later to do a clinic introducing to the Hawaiian culture a more psychological approach to horsemanship, rather than the traditional coercive techniques that were in use. The horse herd had now been reduced to 1,100 head, but the same number of cowboys were still employed. My efforts were quite unsuccessful. The paniolos could not identify with a college-educated man from California that had "Doctor" in front of his name. Two years later, however, buckaroo Ray Hunt went to Parker Ranch and accomplished what I had failed to do; that was to introduce the revolution in horsemanship. Perhaps I had paved the way for his success. The ranch was still running approximately 45,000 head of cattle at that time. The numbers varied from year to year, depending upon the rainfall and available feed.

Another decade passed, and I returned again to do another clinic. The ranch was still running the same number of cattle, and fifty-six cowboys still tended them, but the horses now numbered only 450 head. Trucks and trailers were used to haul horses to the area where they were needed. Mechanization was replacing the horse here.

By the 1980s when I again visited the ranch, the same number of cattle were being run, but now thirty cowboys were employed and the horses numbered 325 head. The cattle herd was the same size a decade later in the 1990s and were worked by twenty-five cowboys. Minimum-wage laws, union labor, and workman's compensation premiums made it expedient to mechanize as much of the operation as possible. Trucks and trailers, motorcycles, helicopters, and all-terrain vehicles facetiously called "Japanese Quarter Horses" were replacing horses.

As I write this chapter, Dr. William "Billy" Bergin, who was for many years the veterinarian for the Parker Ranch, tells me that today twelve cowboys work the ranch, and the horse herd numbers 150 head. Down from 3,000 to 150 in less than half a century! The ranch has been selling off land for development. This has reduced the cattle herd to 25,000 at this time.

Dr. Bergin has written two books thus far chronicling the history of this ranch: *Loyal to the Land—The Legendary Parker Ranch* (2004) tells the history of the area from the years 750 AD to 1950 AD. Volume II, *Loyal to the Land—The Senior Stewards* (2006) relates the history from 1950 to 1970. A third volume is planned. The publisher is the University of Hawaii Press.

The trend toward mechanization is being seen on many large American ranches except where the desire and the pride to do as much of the work as possible on horseback still exist. Mechanization will not completely eliminate the need for ranch horses because rough terrain and relatively wild cattle necessitate good horses.

Interestingly, I once visited a half-million-acre ranch in Kenya that ran 10,000 head of cattle. Right on the equator, but at an average elevation of one mile above sea level, the ranch looked like typical Southwestern range in the United States. It consisted of semi-arid grasslands with scattered thorny trees and riparian draws and canyons. There wasn't a cow horse on the ranch. Why? This was Africa, and native herders lived with the cattle. Each herder had a dozen or two head in his care. When a calf was born, he handled it before the cow did. Thus, the calves were imprinted by him. The ranch manager used that very term, "imprinted." The cattle, handsome Brahman hybrids, saw the native herder as herd leader, and followed him to new grass, to water, and even through the tick-dipping vats. At night, the herder and his cattle retired to a thorn-enclosed "*boma*" to protect the herd from lions and other predators. I learned that cattle ranching can be done without the use of horses, but it is highly improbable that this method will be seen in North America.

We lack the natives that Africa has, who have herded cattle on foot for many centuries, and who are paid far less per day than an American farm worker earns in an hour. It isn't likely that U.S. federal laws will permit workers to wade through tick dip either.

The exploding numbers of horses in America competitively team penning cattle, cutting cattle, and being used in rodeo events can be explained not because of necessity, but because owning, riding, and competing on horses is the greatest joy to so many human beings. The true working horse is a disappearing phenomenon, except for the one described in chapter twenty-three.

CHAPTER TWENTY-TWO

The Warhorse

Look back at our struggle for freedom
Take our present day's strength to its source
You will find Man's pathway to glory
Strewn with the bones of a horse.
　　　　　　　　　　—Author unknown

Of all the working horses that ever existed, no story is more poignant, more dramatic, and more tragic than that of the warhorse.

Without the warhorse, civilization would be many centuries behind where it is today. Indeed, civilizations, such as in the New World, that lacked the horse were greatly restricted in their progress as compared to the Eurasian civilizations, which spread rapidly and influenced one another.*

The warhorse sped the distribution of human culture, technology, and genes. There is no species to which mankind owes a greater debt than to the horse. The hordes of Genghis Khan, of the Roman legions, of Alexander the Great, of Napoleon, all moved via horsepower. War is mankind's greatest folly. Untold millions of humans have died in

---

* The role of the horse and other domestic animals in the progress of Eurasian civilization is vividly chronicled in Jared Diamond's book *Guns, Germs, and Steel: A Short History of Everybody for the Last 13,000 Years* first published in the UK by Chatto & Windus, 1997 (Vintage, 1998, USA Edition).

mankind's wars. More than 60,000 casualties occurred at the Battle of Waterloo. More than 16 million perished in World War I, and between 50 and 55 million died in World War II.

One of several books that chronicle the use of the horse in warfare from ancient times to World War II, The Military Horse *was published by A.S. Barnes & Company, Inc. of Cranbury, New Jersey in 1976. This was the American edition. The original publisher was Marshal Cavendish, Ltd., of Great Britain. This is the cover painting.*

However, mankind has options that the horse never had: surrender, retreat, suicide, or negotiation (by which most wars end). Or, mankind can make the conscious decision to risk dying for a cause. Horses were never given a choice, and they died in incalculable millions.

NAPOLEON'S HORSES

In September of 1812, Napoleon Bonaparte occupied Moscow, Russia, with 600,000 troops, anticipating an easy victory. Like Adolf Hitler in the following century, he underestimated both the determination of the Russians to defend their homeland and the severity of the Russian winter.

Only 25,000 of Napoleon's soldiers made it back to France. Defeated, he had lost almost the entire army of some half million men. He had also lost 160,000 cavalry horses, nearly all that he had brought. Many were killed in battle. Huge numbers simply starved to death. The freezing troops opened the bellies of the dead horses and crawled inside to take refuge from the cold.

The loss of those trained cavalry horses was a military blow that was never corrected. Napoleon returned from exile on the island of Elba in 1815, reformed an army of French supporters, and tried to regain his former status as the conqueror of the civilized world.

He met the armies of Europe, led by the British general Wellington, at the Battle of Waterloo on June 18, 1815.

As the allied cavalry charged Napoleon's positions, they did not realize that a sunken road lay between them and the enemy. The horses plunged over the edge of the road and fell. The struggling bodies of horses and men piled up and were riddled with shots from the French forces. Nevertheless, Napoleon went to his final defeat that day. In 1979, I visited the Waterloo battlefield. On top of a hill, there is a visitor center. Its walls hold a painted mural of the battle. Its windows look down upon a peaceful countryside, unchanged from that awful day.

An English-speaking guide told us the story of the Battle of Waterloo. "More than sixty thousand men died that day, and many thousands of horses," he said. And then, he added (and I chilled at his words), "you are standing on their graves, for they are buried beneath this hill."

Even in World War II, that most mechanized and high-tech war, millions of horses suffered and died. World War II began in 1939 when Nazi Germany invaded Poland. The Polish cavalry, 20,000 strong, vainly tried to stop the onslaught. They were slaughtered, charging tanks with lances. When Germany invaded the Soviet Union, they did it with 740,000 horses and mules, and 4,300 veterinarians. Horse hospitals were right behind the front lines. Both sides lost a thousand horses a day.

Germany used 2.5 million horses in World War II. Half of Germany's transport was horse drawn. The Soviet Union used 3 million. The Germans confiscated horses in every country they invaded. The Soviet Union lost 22 million people during the war, 8 million troops and the rest civilians. The Eastern front was 1,500 miles long.

In August of 1941 the Soviets invaded Finland. The gunfire started a forest fire, and thousands of horses ran into a lake. The next morning the lake was frozen over, with thousands of horse heads stuck above the ice. A few in the shallows were still alive.

At one point, the Germans surrounded two Cossack cavalry divisions. Each Russian killed his own horse. Twelve thousand dead horses blanketed the ground.

The Germans were surrounded at Stalingrad and ordered by Hitler to fight to the death.

They killed 32,000 horses to keep the Soviets from using them. Each soldier was required to shoot his own horse.

Bulgaria had a division of cavalry fighting on the Nazi side. Both horses and men were annihilated.

An Italian division also fought with the Germans. They were almost completely horse drawn, including cavalry and artillery. When Germany retreated from Russia, the food supplies were reserved for the Germans and the Italians had to eat their own horses. Very few men survived.

Toward the end of the war, a German cavalry division was ordered into Budapest as the Soviets advanced. Of 22,000 troops, only 650 survived. None of the horses did.

In the North African campaign, General George Patton pleaded with superiors for cavalry and pack animals. There were none, but he was able to form some pack units using captured Italian horses and packers.

In the war in the Pacific, the Chinese used more than 20,000 horses and mules, often successfully against the Japanese. When Japan invaded China, before America entered the war, it did so with four cavalry brigades.

On March 15, 1942, an American cavalry unit on Bataan killed the last of 250 horses and 48 mules for food.

Early in the war, the U.S. Army phased out the mounted cavalry that had served so well up to that time. However, in both the Pacific and the European theaters of war, the U.S. military continued to use pack mules. They served nobly in the mountainous terrain of Asia and Italy.

After World War II ended, the U.S. Army had thousands of mules overseas in both the European and Pacific theaters of war. Many of these were brought home. Some were used for many years to carry tourists down into the Grand Canyon. Fifteen thousand animals in Europe, mostly mules, were turned over to the United Nations by the U.S. Army and distributed to farmers in war-torn nations. During the aftosa (foot and mouth disease) epidemic campaign in Mexico during the post war years, the U.S. government killed thousands of oxen to keep the disease from entering the United States. These oxen were replaced with ex–U.S. Army mules. Sadly, great numbers of the mules used in the Pacific war were simply transported out to sea, shot, and thrown overboard. They were lamented by their dedicated soldier caretakers.

In 1991, I was invited to San Antonio, Texas to address U.S. Army officers. The Gulf War was in progress, and as an equine veterinarian, and a mule breeder and trainer, I was asked whether I thought mules had a future place in the U.S. Army.*

I told the Desert Storm officers that although I saw no use for mules in the flat desert terrain in the Gulf War occurring at that time, I believed that it was a mistake to completely discontinue military pack mule technology. I pointed out that Stinger Missiles had shot down more than 1,100 Soviet helicopters in that country's unsuccessful attempts to subdue

---

* I don't think they knew that in 1945 I had requested and had been granted a transfer to the Tenth Mountain Division, which had performed so heroically in Italy. The reason I wanted to serve in the Tenth was because I wanted to work with equines. The horses were gone. Only the mules were left. I was eighteen years of age and I also wanted to learn to ski. The Tenth was a ski troop division.

The fighting ended before my transfer was implemented, so I never did get to serve in that unit.

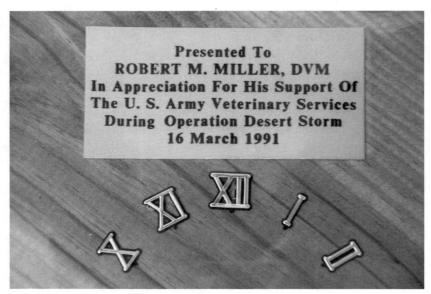

The plaque on the clock I received during Operation Desert Storm.

Afghanistan. The missiles were packed into the mountains on mules. Both the mules and the missiles were supplied to the Afghan Mujahideen by the United States.

I told them that I believed America's future wars would probably involve "brush fire" operations in steep, rugged terrain where pack mules are still more efficient than machines for transporting equipment and supplies.

I reminded them that the U.S. Marine Corps still had a small pack mule training operation in the Sierra Nevada Mountains west of Bridgeport, California, and that many of Europe's modern armies—Germany and Italy, for example—still had mountain warfare mule units.

My presentation was well received, but obviously ignored. I did receive a nice plaque on a clock, which now hangs on my office wall.

In the more recent Afghan and Iraqi wars, and the ongoing war against Islamic terrorism, my prediction proved correct. The American military has had to use locally obtainable horses and mules, and improvise in some of the campaigns. America faces an enemy it has never before had to confront, religious fanaticism, and I foresee a very prolonged war against these zealots. Much of it would be conducive to the use of pack mules.

○ ○ ○

At Bishop Mule Days, California's uniquely Western celebration and show held every May, for several years an old, but still sound mule participated wearing a U.S. Army brand. The last time she appeared she would have been at least fifty years of age as determined by the date of the brand, and she could have been as old as fifty-two.

So, while I believe that the surefooted mule still has a function in modern warfare, the warhorse as we knew it for millennia is obsolete . . . except in one area: mounted police.

CHAPTER TWENTY-THREE

The Last Warhorse

Why does the police horse belong in a book that explains the scientific principles of natural horsemanship?

It is because the police horse is the "last warhorse," and the training methods by which a horse can learn to face rioting and charging crowds, explosions, and violent stimuli of all kinds utilize all the principles of natural horsemanship.

When the internal combustion engine largely displaced the horse, formerly mounted police became dependent upon mechanical means of transportation. Police cars and motorcycles replaced the horse. However, as the twentieth century progressed, a primarily agrarian society became a largely urbanized society. Today more than 90 percent of Americans live in large cities. Even more significant, by the start of the current century, more than half the population on this overcrowded planet lived in large cities.

When I was a child, even big-city children were exposed to concepts of rural life in school. Textbooks were still vestigial remnants of nineteenth-century culture. So many of the stories were about cows and chickens and other farm animals. Kids knew from where milk and eggs came. Today's urban populations are cut off from the agrarian culture that feeds them. As globalization rapidly progresses, more and more of their food and supplies come from far-off places. They live in a very different world.

Although a majority of these city people admire horses, few of them have ever had close contact with a horse. Hence, they fear horses. A policeman on horseback is therefore intimidating, whereas one in a car or on foot may not be.

An experience in the late 1960s, at the height of the counterculture revolution, forever affected my view of the police horse. It was a warm evening in May, and I was in New York City for a national veterinary convention. We visited Greenwich Village where thousands of "flower children" and "hippies" were peacefully congregated at a major intersection. To a country animal doctor, the crowd was both bewildering and exotic.

From a side street came three mounted police officers, riding seventeen-hand, handsome, collected bay geldings. As they approached the crowded square, they turned their horses sideways and slowly side-passed forward, occupying most of the width of the street. One officer, a sergeant, quietly said, "Okay, folks, let's move along! Let's not block traffic! Please, move along folks! Keep moving! There you go!"

The crowd melted away before the three riders. Once in the intersection, they continued their advance, slowly pushing the crowd out of their way and into the several streets that fed into the square.

Suddenly, a girl perhaps sixteen or seventeen years of age ran out from the retreating crowd. She had long, pressed blonde hair, a ring of daisies around her forehead, an ankle-length dress, and bare feet. I thought she was going to spit upon the officers. Instead, she stopped in front of the sergeant's horse, kissed it on the muzzle, and then ran back into the crowd.

Had those officers driven up in police cars, I am sure that they would have been greeted with screams of "Pigs!" and a barrage of bottles and cans. From that moment forward I have become an enthusiast for mounted police units used for crowd control.

The same year that I was in Greenwich Village, a large "hippie" encampment occupied the valley floor in Yosemite National Park. Illicit drug use was rampant and many in the crowd became unruly. A group of poorly trained officers, most of them mounted on Quarter Horses fifteen hands or shorter in height, charged the crowd to disperse it. They were mobbed and many of them were pulled off their horses and beaten.

Police horses ideally need to be no less than sixteen hands in height. The training of these horses must be superb—equal to that of the finest warhorses in history. A police officer on a "bombproof" horse, towering over an urban mob, has a tremendous psychological advantage. I will never forget the response I had to a line of Royal Canadian Mounted Police charging toward me with lowered lances in an exhibition held in a rodeo arena. I'm not afraid of horses, but my adrenalin surged as that line raced toward me. No wonder successful cavalry charges caused enemy lines to falter and break.

Many fine, well-trained and equipped mounted police units exist in the United States. Unfortunately, however, a majority of the nation's mounted police do not have the advantage of ideal horses and optimum training, nor do they receive the financial support they need.

I live in Ventura County, California, a county that is as large as some Eastern states. Half of it is mountain wilderness or national forest. The southern half, however, is growing rapidly, with some of the communities becoming suburbs of adjacent Los Angeles County. Four or five cities have populations of approximately 100,000 people. There are not yet any "big" cities. Therefore, crowd control situations are minimal. We don't have rioting mobs, huge parades, or radical demonstrations.

The Ventura County Mounted Enforcement Unit is a branch of the County Sheriffs' Department. It is budgeted for nineteen officers, but at the time of this writing only twelve are on the force. They all volunteer for mounted duty and provide their own horses. The county supplies trucks and trailers for their use and tack for the horses, but otherwise, there is no direct financial support. The officers meet once a month for training sessions. They prefer Quarter Horses in solid colors, fourteen to sixteen hands in height.

They sometimes patrol shopping malls and parking lots, but much of their duties require backcountry patrols. Drug raids and motorcycle rallies require their services. Their limited crowd control duties include the Ventura County Fair and the Conejo Valley Days celebration in the community where I live. The crowds sometimes become "over-exuberant," according to Captain Chris Lathrop, the officer leading the unit.

This kind of mounted police unit is quite different from the New York City Police Department's units described earlier.

○ ○ ○

Some regions have a need for both the NYPD type of mounted unit and the Ventura County type. Take for example, the huge, sprawling megalopolis of Los Angeles. The city of Los Angeles has densely populated areas, and there is frequent need for police officers and horses that are well trained in crowd control methods. On the other hand, Los Angeles has a lot of rustic areas within the city limits including Griffith Park, the nation's largest urban park. Patrolling such open spaces on horseback involves such extremes as the capture of sex offenders, pursuing runaway rental stable horses with terrified riders aboard, and searches for missing persons and for illegal drug activities.

Dale Rickards was a member of the Los Angeles Police Department for twenty-seven years, twenty of those years in the mounted unit. Now retired, he was a U.S. Army cavalry trooper before becoming a policeman. Based on his experience in the LAPD, he believes the best candidate for a police horse is a ten- or twelve-year-old ranch horse. He believes that there is a place for mounted units to work together with police dogs. The combination of policeman, horse, and dog, all well trained, forms a very effective trio for law enforcement.

Officer Dale Rickards, street patrol, Los Angeles, 1956.

Officer Dale Rickards, park patrol, 1965.

The LAPD has fine stables and horse facilities for its mounted officers and their horses.

The thirty to forty horses are the result of generous endowments by private citizens. The city of Los Angeles contributes little to the costs of maintaining a police unit so vital in the control of unruly crowds.

The *county* of Los Angeles has within its borders not only a megalopolis, one of the world's largest, but also vast areas of mountain, desert, and forested wilderness. The LA County Sheriffs' Department, therefore, also has mounted units. It began as a volunteer organization in 1982, and presently has both volunteer and reserve units.

As is the case in most of the nation's police departments, the officers supply their own horses, the county contributing very little other than administrative expenses.

Rod Bergen has been a mounted officer with the Los Angeles Sheriffs' Department for many years. He is a horsemanship clinician and has extensive experience in training police horses, and also in training recreational horses to be as steady, safe, and reliable as police horses.

Los Angeles County Sheriff's Dept. desensitizing horses to smoke and other hazards.

He says, "Every horse *should* be trained the way police horses *must* be trained." Properly trained police horses must be thoroughly desensitized to fire trucks, ambulance sirens, helicopters, raging crowds, flags, umbrellas, gunfire, smoke bombs, and many other kinds of frightening stimuli.

The duties of the sheriffs' horses are diverse. They accompany the annual Rose Parade, perform search and rescue missions, and do crowd control where needed. During a recent West Hollywood parade, ten mounted officers quickly, quietly, and peacefully cleared the streets after the parade ended.

Los Angeles County Sheriff's Dept. desensitizing police horses to a helicopter.

The urbanization of societies is occurring all over the world, and the usefulness of well-trained mounted police units is being widely recognized. In recent TV news broadcasts I have seen mobs dispersed by mounted police who were obviously very competent and well mounted in England by the London police, in the Gaza Strip by Israeli police, in Paris by French police officers, and in Sydney by Australian officers. These are four of the best trained units in the world.

We see an increasing effectiveness of mounted law enforcement officers in our crowded cities, at events drawing huge audiences, in patrolling our state and national parks and our nation's borders. The authorities and the tax-paying public must be convinced of the value of the equine police units.

○ ○ ○

Dennis Reis, one of the best-known clinicians active in the revolution in horsemanship, has worked with the San Francisco mounted police and many other law enforcement organizations. He conducts police-horse training classes at his ranch near Penngrove, in Northern California. His training of police horses includes desensitizing them to helicopters to the point where they are unafraid of them landing close by. They will even go right up to a helicopter with its engines running and touch it with their muzzles.

Unfortunately, with the exception of such magnificently trained police units as the New York Police Department, most of the nation's mounted police units are hindered in their ability to offer maximum service by bad attitudes held by both the governmental bureaucracy that controls the unit and by the mounted officers themselves. Let's consider these separately:

1. The Bureaucracy

Most city officials, whether elected or appointed, and whether part of the police department or separate from it, are not horsemen. They cannot identify with the officers' desire to work with horses, nor do they appreciate how valuable well-trained units can be. They understand *dogs*, because they are familiar with dogs. They support canine police units in spirit and financially.

Lexington, Kentucky police horse in training. Note the lack of a bridle.

But, these officials take advantage of the officers' eagerness to be mounted. They too often impose the care of the horses, and the cost of maintaining the horse, on the police officers who own the horses.

They do not understand the extensive training that is required to produce an ideal mounted officer and an ideal police horse. They assume that an occasional lesson by somebody whom they consider to be a trainer is adequate. They just do not understand.

2. The Rider's Image

Too often the police officers have hindered themselves by clinging to a cowboy image. Although this is more prevalent in the western United States, it exists everywhere.

Mounted police officers must understand that they are a military force. Cowboys do not enforce the law. Cavalry enforces law. Mounted police must maintain a *military* image.

Tremendous controversies exist within the mounted police units about head gear. Many insist on Stetsons, which is ridiculous! Mounted officers should wear helmets. Why in the world would a mounted officer on a horse not wear a helmet? The helmet not only protects the officer

Lexington, Kentucky police horse in training. Note the Parelli "carrot stick."

from injuries caused by mishaps due to the horses, but also from objects thrown at him by crowds. What is most important is that the helmet *commands* an authoritative air. It has the *military* look.

Police officers who crave a cowboy look don't want *tall* horses. They want a nice stockhorse-sized mount. That is not a good idea. The higher above the crowd the officer is, the more effective. I don't think the Quarter Horse is the ideal police horse, except, perhaps, for rural or backcountry use. In the city you want a tall horse, with a naturally high head carriage, beautifully collected, and its head flexed at the poll. This is imposing—it is intimidating—it is impressive. It commands respect.

Of course, we *all* want the classical Quarter Horse temperament, calm and unperturbed.

However, *any* breed of horse can have that temperament if properly trained using natural horsemanship methods.

○ ○ ○

I was once caught in a hopelessly gridlocked traffic jam in Manhattan. My taxi's driver opened his door, stood up, and leaned on the horn. Every other driver in that gridlock was doing the same thing. The noise was deafening.

"Why are you blowing your horn?" I asked the cab driver.

"It makes me *feel* better," he shouted.

I had only a couple of blocks to walk to my destination, so I paid the driver and got out of the stalled cab. Along came a solitary NYPD mounted officer threading his way through the chaos on his tall, calm, collected, perfectly mannered horse. I stopped to watch as he patiently directed traffic and unglued the gridlock. The horse never flinched, its eyes soft and calm despite the din around it.

"Now, *there's* a police horse!" I thought.

Dennis Reis calls them "battle horses." He points out that dressage maneuvers were taught of military necessity. An ideal police horse must be dressage trained.

Dale Rickards, like Dennis, is a former cowboy. He admits that constantly mounting and dismounting tall horses is hard work. It's also hard for police officers to peer into automobiles from a taller horse. But he agrees that big horses are more effective in controlling crowds. He, too, believes that mounted police officers should convey a military image. "Police horses and the officers who ride them must be taught cavalry maneuvers," says Dale. "Crowds retreat when officers ride stirrup to stirrup."

He says that even in peaceful crowds, the horse unites the officer with the public. People rarely go up to chat with police officers in big city environments. But let the police be astride horses and all kinds of people will come up to pet the horses, smile, and ask questions. The French Quarter in New Orleans on a crowded evening is a good example of this. People stop to look at the police horses, to stroke them, and to talk to the officers.

Rod Bergen says, "Urban crowds are friendly to cops on horseback, whereas they ignore or evade them if the cops are on foot." He says that despite his efforts and the efforts of other enlightened horsemen, most police horse training is *not* done correctly. They are not using fast and effective natural horsemanship methods because in their minds, "it isn't cowboy." This mindset prevails, despite the fact that the entire revolution in horsemanship was initiated by a handful of cowboys from the Pacific Northwest.

CHAPTER TWENTY-FOUR

The Evolution of Horsemanship

Yes, you read the title of this chapter correctly. I said "evolution," not "revolution." In a half century I have witnessed an amazing change in the way horses are handled and I want to describe the extremes of that change.

In chapter thirteen I briefly described my first experience starting a colt in 1948 under the supervision of a professional "horse breaker." Let me describe in more detail the process of how ranch colts were "broken" over a half century ago. Sadly, the method still exists today. The colt back then was at least four years of age when first roped, although the one I was given to break was only three. It may have been roped around the neck using a rope that was "dallied" (wound around) a snubbing post in the center of the round corral and the colt was then choked down. In some cases the colt was roped by the forelegs with a loop we called "*mangana*" or "*mangana de pie*," and then tripped and thrown. This was also called "fore-footing."

In either case, one man then held the head in such a manner that the colt couldn't rise. If the colt was still on its feet, it was then "eared down." That was my job with Pintado, the first colt I started. The ears were grasped and pulled downward and the tip of one ear was bitten by the handler's teeth. This usually immobilized the colt long enough to get it blindfolded, the forelegs hobbled, and the left hind leg "scotched up." That is, it is tied up so that the colt is standing on three legs. What I am describing is well known to every person from a cowboy background who is, at present, past middle age. It was that common. The "earing" of a horse, although crude and risky, is effective.

I remember, as a boy in the 1930s, seeing a documentary movie about the capture of wild animals in Africa. In one scene, zebra were pursued in a truck. A loop of rope attached to a pole was snared around the neck of one zebra. The truck was then stopped and while the zebra fought the choking rope two natives ran up to it. One native grabbed the ears and bit down on one. The zebra stopped struggling, allowing the second native to quickly hobble its legs. Obviously, this method of physically restraining Equidae has been used in many different parts of the globe and of necessity often is still used by professional horse handlers to restrain a horse.

Whether fore-footed or snubbed, the unbroken colt was forcibly restrained until a halter or a hackamore could be placed on its head. Next, the colt was "sacked out." It was repeatedly struck with a blanket or a gunny sack until there was no longer any resistance. This is the flooding technique described earlier. It works, and most colts, although terrified, are soon habituated to this particular stimulus.

The colt was then saddled. The "stomper," "bronc rider," or "peeler" then climbed aboard. The blindfold was lifted and the hobbles released. Although my first colt didn't buck, most did and often violently. Eventually, the bucking stopped and the colt was now "broken" to the saddle and to the rider.

Similar methods are used in Latin America, Australia, and in Canada.

Amazingly, it works most of the time. A majority of the colts started this way turn out to be useful, tractable horses, although a high percentage will often "break in two" (start bucking), often with no warning and with little provocation. Some, of course, will never submit and are designated as "outlaws."

This is the time-honored cowboys' method. It was fast, but not a good way to create a completely trustworthy horse. Many horses were injured in this process. So were many men. Some of each died, but it was a method born of frontier necessity. Horses were cheap, and so were cowboys.

The ritual has been preserved and celebrated in countless works of art, in books, in movies, and on the Wyoming license plate. It took skill

The logo that adorns the Wyoming license plate.

and courage on the part of the men who did this work. It gave birth to the sport of rodeo.

But—in the light of present knowledge, and the demonstrable results of the revolution in horsemanship, this method was unnecessarily crude. It was brutal. And, it did not encourage optimum results.

Since 2003, a colt-starting competition has been held annually called Road to the Horse. Before a large audience, a few clinicians are allowed a total of three hours over a weekend to start an unbroken colt. In between the training sessions, various educational or entertainment events are presented. At the conclusion of the three hours of work with the colts the contestants must take them through an obstacle course to prove their progress, and finally, they have the option of a freestyle demonstration to do whatever they think will favorably impress the judges.

The first of these competitions was held in Fort Worth, Texas, featuring clinicians Josh Lyons, Curt Pate, and Clinton Anderson. When I was asked to be one of the five judges, I was hesitant about accepting the invitation. I don't like conflict and I was concerned that differences of opinion amongst the five judges could result in disagreement. My dislike of conflict is one reason I became a user of natural horsemanship in my early twenties. I didn't like fighting horses.

Ten two-year-old colts, broken only to lead and otherwise unstarted, were supplied by an Arkansas ranch. The judges were to select three of the colts as similar to one another as possible for the three contestants. The judges were not permitted to confer with one another on their choices. Five of the colts were sired by one stallion and were reasonably similar. The other five, all sired by a Hancock sire, were even more similar. I

The 2006 Road to the Horse competition in the Miller Arena, Murfreesboro, Tennessee.

promptly limited my choice to those five. Observing the horses at liberty I soon picked out the most dominant individual, and conversely the most submissive individual. Eliminating those two, I was left with the three Hancock colts in the middle. They were my choice. All five judges came up with the same three colts. My apprehensions about conflict disappeared. I now regard my fellow judges at Road to the Horse with the utmost respect and affection.

Clinton Anderson didn't get on his horse until the second day. Careful preparation for the finale won the contest when he did his performance.

○ ○ ○

The next Road to the Horse was held in a coliseum in Murfreesboro, Tennessee, before an audience of six thousand people, this time featuring two Texas clinicians, Van Hargis and Craig Cameron, and once again the young Australian, Clinton Anderson, who won the competition a second time. However, the judges and the audience agreed that there were no "losers." All three competitors did a fine job and won a standing ovation.

Again held in Murfreesboro before a huge audience, the 2006 competition was different. The colts this time were not two-year-olds.

They were all three- and four-year-olds. Every colt starter knows how much more submissive and tractable a two-year-old is than a three- or four-year-old. With maturity, horses become more willful and difficult. For the first time none of the colts were halter broken. They were wild.

In addition to three very experienced and very competent cowboys—Texans Craig Cameron and Van Hargis, and Idaho buckaroo Martin Black—a fourth clinician had been added. Stacy Westfall, a woman, had entered the competition. She was a petite mother of three children all under the age of six. An experienced horsewoman, Stacy had an impressive list of achievements, especially in reining. Her mentors included top show trainers and such clinicians as Pat Parelli.

What happened was so unexpected, and so dramatic, that it belongs in this book on natural horsemanship.

Of eight unbroken colts, the judges selected four pairs consisting of what was felt were an easier colt, and a more challenging one. Each competing clinician was then free to choose either colt of a pair that they had drawn. Stacy chose the colt I thought was the most difficult of the eight, a rather wild-eyed three-and-a-half-year-old. Two of the other judges later told me that they, too, thought she had selected the most difficult colt.

At the end of the first day's work of an hour and a half, she seemed to have accomplished very little. All that she had been able to do was to put a halter on her colt and bridle it. Most of the audience probably thought Stacy was wasting her time. It also looked like Martin Black, a superb horseman, was going to be an easy winner. He and one of the other men had already been on their horses' backs. Martin had his colt haltered five minutes after he began working with him, saddled in less than ten minutes, and he was in the saddle less than fifteen minutes after the event began.

In retrospect, what I believe happened is that Stacy had not created fear in her horse. Quietly moving it around, she had established her dominance, with the colt beginning to see her as a herd leader to be trusted, and not to be feared.

The men—and I want to emphasize what excellent horsemen all three were—pushing the envelope a bit because of the time constraints and the competitive atmosphere, had certainly gained the respect of their colts, but the relationship was not devoid of fear.

Stacy Westfall, the unexpected winner and the bronc she named Popcorn.

The next day, a dramatic change could be seen in Stacy's colt. It had softened and relaxed to a remarkable degree. Before long she had it saddled and was trotting and loping it in the round pen.

Later when the pens were dismantled and the colts were presented with the obstacle course in an open arena, the men's colts balked, bucked, shied, and bolted. They were fearful! Stacy rode her horse through the course competently and smoothly, to the amazement of the spectators, event organizers, and all five judges. She won the Road to the Horse competition.

What happened was the essence of what we call natural horsemanship—to shape the behavior of the horse and dominate it, not with coercion or force or pain or fear, but rather with persuasion, bonding, dependence, desensitization, and operant conditioning. If the goal in the horse–human relationship is 100 percent trust and respect, and zero fear, that is what Stacy accomplished in Murfreesboro, Tennessee, in 2006.

Not to be misunderstood, I am not saying that causing fear in a horse at any time is wrong or destructive. In working with horses, especially young green horses, it is inevitable that fear occurs in this flighty subject. The rapid fear response is what keeps horses alive in the wild. The secret of overcoming the fear response is repetition until habituation (most clinicians call this desensitization) sets in.

When I flood a newborn foal with various sensory stimuli, it is at first terrified. With repetition, the fear subsides, habituation occurs, and indifference to or even enjoyment of the stimulus may occur. Similarly, when "sacking out" a colt, if we were to stop prematurely while the flight response is still present, we have *rewarded* flight. Thus, we fix that response. On the other hand, if we persist in the stimulus until the desire for flight is gone we have effectively desensitized the horse to that particular stimulus. What happens in a colt-starting competition is that *haste* results in certain stimuli being abandoned before habituation has occurred. The colt is then programmed to flight when that stimulus is experienced again. Stacy's prolonged, soft, low-key approach the first day extinguished a lot of the flight response in her colt.

Keep in mind that although I was a judge, I was also a spectator. Looking back upon what I have seen in my lifetime, the extremes in horsemanship make the revolution a very *real* revolution.

I described how colts were started when I was young. All that crude brutality, the danger to both horse and human, the intellectual shallowness of it, was not because the men working with those colts were intentionally cruel. They weren't; they just did not know a better way.

Now we know a better way. Road to the Horse–type contests are not intended to encourage people to use a "quickie" method to train horses. They simply demonstrate how much can be accomplished in a very short time if scientifically sound behavior shaping and behavior modifying methods are properly used. All of the clinicians advise taking all the time necessary, and being patient while using the gentler methods they advocate.

I saw the ultimate in crude horsemanship when I was young. Now, in old age, I am humbly grateful that I have lived long enough to see these changes and to see this timid, flighty, useful prey animal treated as it deserves to be treated, with kindness, with firm gentleness, with affection and respect.

In a world in which every news broadcast and every newspaper is filled with stories of horrific crimes of terrorism, of immoral acts and unethical offenses, this revolution in horsemanship offers a ray of hope to mankind. Civility, being considerate of others, intelligent communication, common courtesy, good manners, and using reason rather than emotion, are more effective than acting like a savage—or a chimpanzee.

CHAPTER TWENTY-FIVE

What Do Horses Mean to Us?

Jared Diamond, author of *Guns, Germs, and Steel,* explains why the civilizations of Eurasia advanced more rapidly than those on the other continents. More extensive temperate zones facilitated agriculture, communication between peoples, and the exchange of technological information. Additionally, the prehistoric people of Eurasia had the advantage of many domestic animals. They had sheep, goats, dogs, cattle, and *horses*. By contrast, Native Americans had only the dog in the Northern hemisphere, and dogs, llamas, and guinea pigs in the Southern hemisphere.

The horse, wherever it was domesticated, gave mankind speed, draft power, and the ability to travel longer distances. Mounted armies spread destruction, but they also spread knowledge, technology, religion, art, and their genes. It is not surprising, therefore, that in every horse-owning culture the beast was glorified, admired, and even deified. Moreover, the *horseman* was similarly glorified and respected.

The word for horse in Latin is *caballus*. Thus, in Spanish *caballero*, a horseman, is synonymous with "gentleman." In English, we have the similar word "cavalier," of French origin. The horse historically represented power and masculinity. The world over, statues depict kings, emperors, generals, and conquerors astride stallions, despite the fact that many of these people rarely or never rode horses. Astride stallions, their roles as leaders, as virile warriors, as *alpha males* was emphasized.

No other domestic animal has served to portray human male dominance to the degree that the horse has, but note that astride the powerful, intimidating stallion, it is the *man* who is in control.

Although the horse has, to some degree, retained its historical role in modern society, it now fills other roles in our psyche. Horses in advertising are used to sell automobiles, beer, and perfume. Now that women dominate the equine industry numerically, the image of the horse meets other and varied psychological connotations. An ad for a product to combat osteoporosis shows an older woman, the wind blowing her hair, with her horse.

Why are women so attracted to horses? Does the horse symbolize masculinity? Is it a fantasy substitute for a male figure, even if the horse is a mare? Does it represent a paternal figure, a mate, or perhaps simply a male dominated by a woman? Perhaps horses can represent all of these elements.

As a practicing veterinarian, I was keenly aware of the nurturing instinct that is so strong in most women and also in many men. This nurturing instinct frequently expresses itself in a love for animals. Many women cannot express that love to horses simply because they live in an area incompatible with horse ownership. Horses are expensive to keep, and many people who would love to have a horse simply cannot afford to own one. One reason the guest ranch industry is burgeoning is because of the increasing urbanization of the nation. The growth of the megalopolis precludes horse ownership. Dude ranches increase in number all over the land, and rental stables can be found in and near every large city.

Rather than because of its image of virility and power, many women are attracted to horses because of the animal's vulnerability. Whereas men have often seen the horse as a big and strong beast to conquer (after all, in our species, the men *hunted* and the women *gathered* food), women are usually perceptive enough to see the horse's timidity. Despite its size and physical strength, the horse is an easily frightened and flighty creature. This vulnerability arouses in women an emotional desire to protect, to reassure, to comfort, and it does in some men as well.

For some of us, enormous gratification is achieved by *conquering* the beast. We survived as a species because our ancestors readily and gleefully attacked and killed all kinds of large animals, including huge herbivores such as the woolly mammoth. Taming a bronc, spurring it and whipping it with a quirt at every jump and successfully riding it until it stops bucking and surrenders, fulfills this primitive instinct for many people.

On the other hand, other people derive just as much satisfaction using natural horsemanship to convert a panicky, terrified colt into a friendly, calm, trusting, and dependent partner.

My wife, who pursued the horse-show circuit and was a very successful barrel racer in the 1950s, says that her successes in those endeavors never brought the satisfaction that using natural horsemanship with her horses has brought her. We are all different. We have different needs. They change with our background, our emotional state, and our age.

I find it very significant that a majority of the original clinicians who began the revolution in horsemanship were ex-rodeo contestants. Most of them, in fact, participated not in the timed events such as steer wrestling or roping in which the horse is a *partner*, but in rough-stock events such as

My wife, Debby, was one of the country's top barrel racers in the 1950s. Seen here in a Texas race, she says nothing in the rodeo or show arena has given her the satisfaction that natural horsemanship has.

bareback and saddle bronc riding, wherein the horse is pitted against the rider. Pat Parelli says that he rode broncs "until his brains came in."

I rather suspect that diminishing testosterone level is the reason that so many of us converted from battling horses to softly mastering them. In either case, there was a love of being near horses and a desire to work with them.

There is an interesting analogy in the contrasting roles that horses play in human lives and the role that historically dominant humans have played. Some of these human leaders achieved dominance through the use of force. Genghis Khan, Alexander the Great, Napoleon Bonaparte, Adolf Hitler, Joseph Stalin, and Saddam Hussein are examples of powerful leaders who achieved and maintained their leadership roles through the use of force.

On the other hand, consider the immensely influential dominant figures in world history who did *not* use coercion to achieve their success, but rather did it with *persuasion*. Among those are Mahatma Gandhi, Aristotle, Socrates, and Martin Luther King, Jr. Is there an example of a more successful individual who used reason and persuasion to achieve dominance than Jesus Christ?

One of the most impressive things I believe George Washington did for our country was to reject royalty and even a third presidential term. Here was a *warrior*, a *successful* warrior, appointed to lead a new nation, yet he was *civilized* enough to reject the role of the alpha male when it was offered.

I have heard the comment too many times that "Natural horsemanship is okay for horses that are to be used for girls and ladies, but not for my horses." Really? If natural horsemanship is designed for wimps, why have Bill Smith (three times PRCA World Champion Saddle Bronc Rider), Larry Mahan (six times PRCA World Champion All Around Cowboy), Mel Hyland (twice PRCA World Champion Bronc Rider), and Ty Murray (nine times PRCA World Champion Rodeo Cowboy) all converted to natural horsemanship? In fact, they all are *clinicians* now teaching the most effective, most humane, most civilized form of horsemanship of all time.

○ ○ ○

A horse is more than a fetish, more than an outlet for a competitive spirit, more than a companion. The marvelous results being obtained with horses as therapy for the physically and mentally impaired speak for themselves. Therapeutic riding programs across the land all testify that extraordinary benefits are occurring. Autistic children communicate. Cerebral palsy victims joyously ride. Paraplegics know the ecstasy of being mobile. It has been credited to many sources including Winston Churchill, Will Rogers, and Ronald Reagan, but no more truthful adage exists than the one that states, "The outside of the horse is good for the inside of a man."

If riding can produce such beneficial results in the physically impaired, improving both their physical effectiveness and their psychological attitude, it helps us to understand why horses are important to so many people. Riding, competing, driving, working, or simply handling horses makes us *feel* better. If we *feel* better, we *are* better. This is the main reason that horses, largely displaced as working animals by twentieth- and twenty-first-century technology, are *increasing* in popularity. They offer us repose; enhance our physical well-being; improve our balance, our coordination, and our confidence; and bring us closer to nature. Of course, this is true of many recreational activities such as hiking, skiing, cycling, kayaking, and so

William Beckett, a child with autism, on Onion, an 8-year-old BLM mustang, assisted by Donna Martin and Bud Lance at H.O.R.S.E.S. Ltd.

on, but the horse offers us an additional benefit. It is a living creature, not an inanimate piece of sports equipment. Intelligent, sensitive, responsive, and often affectionate, the horse can be a companion, a friend. A bicycle can't be that. I love to ski, but I don't have a personal, living relationship with my skis. I do with my horses. Well, actually I should say my "half-horses" because now I have more mules than horses.

Sure, I love my skis, but if anybody saw me talking to them, stroking them, and hugging them, I supposed they'd think I was a potential psychiatric patient. If my skis *returned* my affection, softly speaking to me, caressing me, and following me around, I'd have to agree with them.

Moreover, my skis don't *need* me. They are content to be in the closet. My animals *need* me. They need me and I need them. They are alive. They experience curiosity, gratification, alarm, fear, pleasure, contentment, fatigue, exhilaration, and excitement, just as people do. They live! That's why they mean so much to those of us fortunate enough to own them.

Kerrill Knaus-Hardy is the president of H.O.R.S.E.S. Ltd. of Scotts Mills, Oregon. A quadriplegic, she rides, as seen here, in a specially constructed saddle, on Czar, a 20-year-old mare. Kerrill's organization is one of many therapeutic riding facilities, which are rapidly increasing in number. She is accompanied by volunteers Todd Rahm (left) and Clint Dern.

EPILOGUE

In the first chapter of this book, I stated that there are two non-traditional aspects to the revolution in horsemanship:

The first is the power of learning early in life—in "childhood" if you will.

The second is the innovation of what we have come to know as "natural horsemanship." Coercive methods come to humans easily and have been the methods traditionally used to shape equine behavior. But now they are being displaced by gentler, kinder, and far more effective persuasive methods that require optimum communication between horse and handler.

The success of the revolution in horsemanship should serve as inspiration for the handling of *all* animals. More importantly, it offers hope for human society.

If all children were reared in a safe, wholesome, and disciplined environment by intelligent, considerate, and well-educated parents, they would probably grow up to be reasonable, happy, and well-motivated adults. Then, as adults, in dealing with their peers, their subordinates, their superiors, and their children, if all methods of coercion were eliminated, and replaced with reason and persuasion, wouldn't this be a far better world?

The revolution in horsemanship has proven in the limited relationship between horses and humans that communication and the power of reason *can* prevail. It offers a hopeful example for all of us.

—RMM

INDEX